More F

RITA F. SNOWD... countries and is books for adult... at business she trained as a deaconess of the New Zealand Methodist Church, serving in turn two pioneer country areas before moving to the largest city for several years of social work during an economic depression.

Miss Snowden has served the world Church, beyond her own denomination, with regular broadcasting commitments. She has written and spoken in Britain, Canada, the United States, in Australia, and in Tonga at the invitation of Queen Salote. She has represented her church at the World Methodist Conference in Oxford; later being elected the first woman Vice-President of the New Zealand Methodist Church, and President of its Deaconess Association. She has served as an Honorary Vice-President of the New Zealand Women Writers' Society, is a Fellow of the International Institute of Arts and Letters, and a member of P.E.N.

Miss Snowden has been honoured by the award of the Order of the British Empire, and by the citation of "The Upper Room" in America.

RITA F. SNOWDEN

More Prayers for Women

Collins
FOUNT PAPERBACKS

First published in Fontana Paperbacks 1975
Second Impression August 1975
Reprinted in Fount Paperbacks January 1977
Seventh Impression May 1988

Printed and bound in Great Britain by
William Collins Sons & Co. Ltd, Glasgow

The Bible readings are from the *Revised Standard Version
Bible*, copyrighted 1946, 1952, and © 1971 by the
Division of Christian Education of the National Council
of the Churches of Christ in the USA and are used by
permission.

CONTENTS

PREFACE

It is easier to write a preface to this second book of prayers for
a woman's use than it was to do as much for the earlier one.
By now many, many thousands the world round know it, and
use it, in its pleasant paper jacket – some of its phrases have
walked up and down in our minds so long that they need a
rest and replacement to spell refreshment. Hence this second
book.

It follows much the same pattern, with prayers in present-
day speech for morning and evening for thirty-one days, with
a reading accompanying each – the Old and New Testaments
alternating. And there are extra pages to cover Sundays for a
month; with a handful of prayers for personal occasions and
particular occupations. A page of new graces is added – one
need not apologize for thinking about food in this hungry
world.

All the Scripture readings are from the Revised Standard
Version – but these are not of set purpose to win you from
your own beloved version – they can be read side by side, and
new light will surely come. The use of a reverent 'you' has
replaced the ancient 'Thou' – but again, if this does not serve
reality for you, revert to the term which comes most naturally
to you. Reality is of such importance. A little patience, none
the less, could reveal something of great worth in this modern-
day usage.

Time passes swiftly and many things in our lives fall out
of use – but we can't afford to let prayer be one of them. We
are made to pray – not because we are specially pious, but
because we are persons in relationship of some kind with the
great eternal person, God. Our approach to prayer these days
might be very different – our posture, our phraseology, the
scope of concerns and people for whom we pray.

Prayer is laying our lives, with all their fascinating interests, obligations and relationships, before God, who already
knows how much each matters. It is not just asking for things

it would be nice to have – easily have – it is desiring, above all, to be in relationship with God, in the way he would like us to be. So it is more than words – however neatly coined our phrases – it is also a matter of listening. And this takes time. We can pray, of course, in a rush, in a crisis – as we run to a human friend on occasion; but a rich and growing friendship takes more than that. Any woman who prays with naturalness and reality knows this. She has long outgrown her childhood, girlhood prayers, though sometimes phrases from them come back into her mind. Prayer is not even remembering fine adult words – though some cherished come fittingly – it is a commitment of one's whole personality.

A regular part of the day kept deliberately for this helps – but we can pray anywhere, at any time, with or without words, though we are, of all creation, word-using creatures, and it helps to clothe our aspirations in words. Until one prays for another – sincerely, imaginatively entering into her life – one can't know what a difference it can make to her and to oneself.

This little book, like its forerunner, is meant to be a stimulus on the way to a new reality.

R.F.S.

PRAYERS
WITH BIBLE READINGS
FOR THIRTY-ONE DAYS

FIRST DAY

In the Morning

O God, it is wonderful to waken in this world spinning in space – and to know that it is your world – and that I am yours.

   I bring you thanks for the renewal of sleep; for the light and life of the sun; for the colours of grass and garden.

   I rejoice in my family relationships; in my friends; in the laughter of little children; in the serenity and wisdom of age.

   I believe that nothing can happen today without you; that people always matter more than things;

   that no human need can out-match your love and power.

In work and leisure this day, grant me an awareness of your nearness –

   where I am weak, O God, make me strong;

   where I am strong, make me gentle;

   and deliver me from pride that so easily spoils things.

Enable me to lend a helping hand to those who carry burdens;

   to share a word of encouragement with the hard-pressed;

   to offer a listening ear to the lonely;

   to set some laughter in the eyes of the weary.

These words of my heart, I offer in the name of Christ. AMEN

FIRST DAY

In the Evening

Gracious Lord, I bring you my thanks that I have not walked alone this day—but have known your presence; that I have enjoyed the support of family and friends; that I have been able to live against the background of many good people.

Forgive me if I have been foolish in my decisions; if I have wasted precious time and energy; if I have thought myself superior to others; if I have been so wrapped up in my own affairs, that I have spared no thought for others.

This has been a long day, and now the wild creatures seek their rest, and I seek mine. Be especially near all who come to this hour with anxiety; all who face illness; all at home, but estranged; all who must face the result of rash actions; especially those in need who fail to pray for themselves. For Christ's sake. AMEN

Daily Reading

Jesus said: 'Believe in God, believe also in me. In my Father's house are many rooms; if it were not so, would I have told you that I go to prepare a place for you? And when I go and prepare a place for you, I will come again, and will take you to myself, that where I am you may be also. And you know the way where I am going.' Thomas said to him, 'Lord, we do not know where you are going; how can we know the way?' Jesus said to him, 'I am the way, and the truth, and the life; no one comes to the Father, but by me.'

John 14:1-6

SECOND DAY

In the Morning

Gracious God, as this day dawns, my first thoughts are toward you — in thanks for life, in thanks for your prophets and preachers and teachers through whom I have learned something of your heart.

Let no failure of my yesterday hold me back from life today — I would accept your forgiveness, I would set aside as best I can my pretence, my pettiness, my stumbling pride.

Grant that my response today may measure up to the claims of love which I make; my work be as true as my words, my courage be unflinching, if I have difficult things to do.

Guard today all whose work is dangerous — quicken in them just care; grant perseverance to all whose work is dull; give them encouragement. Grant your special care to all who start out on new work today.

Give wisdom and foresight to the world's peace-makers — some known to me by name, some often named in the newspapers, some unknown, as they work in countries ravaged by war, disrupted by hate, full of suffering.

All who work patiently with refugees;
all who meet with the injured and harassed;
all who spend their time in councils and conferences.

Grant to those who report for the world's reading and hearing, good sense, truth and justice, that things may be seen in perspective — newspaper people, broadcasters, TV reporters.

Scatter the secret designs of all set on frustration, violence, and fear, that the peoples of the world may come to a better day of understanding and mutual helpfulness. In Christ's name, and the service of your kingdom.

AMEN

SECOND DAY

In the Evening

From time beyond human remembrance, O God, men and women have hushed their hearts to pray at the day's end – and I do that now:

    here let me shed my haste;

    here let me know deep honesty;

    here let me lay fresh hold on your love.

    Encourage all that has been good in me today; correct with tenderness all my error; keep me teachable as I reflect on this.

    If I have stilled my conscience, forgive me;

    if I have prided myself on my accomplishments, forgive me.

I praise you for my favourite books, that have shown me fresh truth –

    have quickened my imagination;

    have taught me to laugh and be free.

I praise you for my favourite composers, and musicians –

    those who have come to me in person;

    those through radio and records.

Especially for my home in which loyalty and love dwells, I give you thanks.

Daily Reading

It is good to give thanks to the Lord,

    to sing praises to thy name, O Most High;

to declare thy steadfast love in the morning,

    and thy faithfulness by night,

to the music of the lute and the harp,

    to the melody of the lyre.

For thou, O Lord, hast made me glad

    by thy work;

at the works of thy hands I sing for joy.

                                Psalm 92 : 1-4

THIRD DAY

In the Morning

O God, send me out into things this day with eagerness, and bring me in at nightfall, unashamed. It is wonderful to be assured that no fresh opportunity comes without your knowledge; no fresh obstacle, without your knowledge.

I give you thanks for the intimate joys of my home; for its happy memories; for its growing relationships;

that no one crosses its doorstep of right, without a loving welcome; that no one seeking laughter and joy, is disappointed;

that here hurts are the concern of all; that here, successes are the natural pride of all.

Let no standards, low in themselves, no things, shoddy in themselves, find here a lodging.

Quicken in me today a love of things beautiful and good and true; and help me to add some piece of worthwhile knowledge to what I have.

Be especially close today to any who bear secret burdens —

to parents of handicapped children;

to teachers of undisciplined scholars;

to social-workers in unattractive surroundings;

to counsellors who must try to save marriages;

to magistrates and judges who must temper the Law with mercy.

Deliver us all from self-love, from intolerance, from over-sureness, and enable us to walk humbly and gladly through the duties and delights of this day — in the spirit of Christ.

AMEN

THIRD DAY

In the Evening

O God, I bring you thanks for the experiences of this day —
  recalling the new people I have met;
  the new ideas which have proved stimulating;
  I give thanks for all who have enriched my living this day —
all who have given me opportunities for service.
  have met my routine needs, grocers, busmen, postmen;
I give thanks for the countless good men and women
  who have passed this way before me;
  who have added colour and excitement to life;
  who have left me a song to sing.
I thank you especially that you have not answered my short-
sighted prayers, but in your infinite wisdom, have led me to
some better thing. I surrender myself — body, mind, and soul.

AMEN

Daily Reading

Who shall separate us from the love of Christ? Shall tribula-
tion, or distress, or persecution, or famine, or nakedness, or
peril, or sword? As it is written, 'For thy sake we are being
killed all the day long; we are regarded as sheep to be
slaughtered.' No, in all these things we are more than con-
querors through him who loved us. For I am sure that neither
death, nor life, nor angels, nor principalities, nor things present, nor things to come, nor powers, nor height, nor depth,
nor anything else in all creation, will be able to separate us
from the love of God in Christ Jesus our Lord.

Romans 8 : 35-39

FOURTH DAY

In the Morning

O God, as I waken safe and sound, I remember all who return to consciousness hungry; all who waken to a day hampered by fears; all who suffer injustice; all who know hurt of body and mind; all robbed of true dignity and joy in life.

I pray for social-workers, and all devoted to planting understanding where none is; establishing fair-dealing where none is; enabling things beautiful and true to flourish in the place of ugliness and damage. Let the sacredness of human personality become clear to many more today; grant wisdom to those who must interpret the Law with strength and mercy; quicken the imagination of those who teach young minds.

Surround with strong friends and wise those who seek strength in drugs; those who feel themselves defeated in life; those with glimmerings of goodness, who would try again. Bless especially all who serve life in great institutions and homes; all who lead young people in wholesome sport; all who write the things that lively minds read; and those who prepare the films and dramas they see.

And bless this day all young couples setting up home; all young parents rejoicing in their little ones; all starting work in the big world of affairs.

So may the standards of Christ — good and true and full of justice and joy — flourish amongst us. So may we serve your Kingdom faithfully — whether anyone about us sees or not; so may we continue our discipleship in high courage. Along with honour, grant us an unwavering sense of humour — in the name of Christ who moved thus amongst men and women in this same earth.   AMEN

FOURTH DAY

In the Evening

For the colours of the sky, and quiet of the world at day's end, I bring my thanks, O God – for all living creatures that seek rest; for little children safely tucked in; for sick people tended with modern skill and ageless compassion; for old people made comfortable and peaceful.

Bless this night all far from home – all who travel by sea, air or road. Bless all whose working hours fall while others sleep – nurses, doctors, firemen, policemen, caretakers. Strengthen their courage, keep them alert and responsible till their tasks are done. Bless especially those whose work is dangerous; those whose work offers small opportunities for advance; those whose work cuts them off from daily fellowship with others. Grant to us all your blessings in our going out, and in our coming in, now and for ever.   AMEN

Daily Reading

Hear the word of the Lord, O people of Israel;
for the Lord has a controversy with the inhabitants of the land.
There is no faithfulness or kindness, and no knowledge of God in the land;
there is swearing, lying, killing, stealing, and committing adultery;
they break all bounds and murder follows murder.
Therefore the land mourns, and all who dwell in it languish,
and also the beasts of the field, and the birds of the air;
and even the fish of the sea are taken away.

Hosea 4:1-3

FIFTH DAY

In the Morning

O Lord God, Eternal Father, utterly to be trusted, I trust you
to guide me through this new day. Let the memories of days
gone strengthen my trust; let the experiences of days gone
guide me in my choices.

I am fascinated by your power to roll back the darkness to
make this day;

I am fascinated by your creative skill with beautiful colours and shapes;

I am fascinated by the song of streams and birds and wild
creatures;

I am fascinated by the patterns of fields, and hedgerows,
and their productiveness;

I am fascinated by the skills of men and women passed
from one to another down the years.

Knowing that my place is in this great on-going stream of
life, I ask for strength to live well today, and to laugh at life's
absurdities.

Let the skills that you have entrusted to me, be used today
for the good of all; save me from coveting the skills or goods
of others.

Grant that the peace for which I pray for the world may
be fashioned in my own little world of affairs.

Bless especially all who are worried; all who have been
deprived of their dues; all who, for lack of living faith, fail
to pray for themselves. AMEN

FIFTH DAY

In the Evening

Eternal Father, save me from taking for granted any of the delights of this day; any of the associations of this day.

Let my recollection of its hours be creative; let my mistakes show me how to approach things better tomorrow.

I worry about my home sometimes; about —— and —— Save me from ever trying to carry burdens alone.

In this quiet place, let me face the things I ought to face, before this day melts into the great on-going pattern of life.

Forgive me if I have been ungenerous in my attitudes today, unforgiving, ungracious.

O Father, my life is a very human mixture of knowledge and ignorance, of kindness and carelessness.

Help me in this quietness, to sort out my priorities, to acknowledge my failings. Quicken my imagination that I may see new ways of doing dull things, and better ways of serving your will in the world. Where I have hesitated at the cross-roads of choice, make me eager to do your bidding with my whole heart. Make this world a better place because I live in the spirit of Christ, to your glory, now and always.   AMEN

Daily Reading

Jesus said: 'Consider the lilies of the field, how they grow; they neither toil nor spin; yet I tell you, even Solomon in all his glory was not arrayed like one of these. But if God so clothes the grass of the field, which today is alive and tomorrow is thrown into the oven, will he not much more clothe you, O men of little faith? Therefore do not be anxious, saying, "What shall we eat?" or "What shall we drink?" or "What shall we wear?" For the Gentiles seek all these things; and your heavenly Father knows that you need them all. But seek first his kingdom and his righteousness, and all these things shall be yours as well.'

Matthew 6:28-33

SIXTH DAY

In the Morning

Lord of life, my heart surges with thankfulness as I waken to
the light of this new day —
> for safe-keeping through the night;
> for bodily comfort and peace of mind;
> for the refreshing miracle of sleep.

Help me today to show a generous attitude to others —
> requiring no higher standards of them than of myself:
> being as patient with lagging steps as you are of mine;
> as ready with forgiveness as you are ready to forgive me.

I pray this day for the protection of the unborn; for all tender
new lives; for the ignorant and inexperienced; for the handicapped in body or mind; for the reckless and careless and the
slow-witted.

Grant your special wisdom and patience to all who have to
deal with these; let them handle with gentleness and knowledge those who make persistent claims upon them. Give them
the patience they need. Enable them to cross to others with
understanding, by any bridge they know.

Have mercy, O God, on all who selfishly exploit others;
all who show superiority, and rob others of dignity and worth.

You have enriched our lives in many unexpected ways;
you have rewarded our small efforts beyond our deserts; you
have held us secure in your love.

Deliver us all this day from moodiness, from irritability,
from quick temper, from cold casualness. Let the spirit of
Jesus be ours. AMEN

SIXTH DAY

In the Evening

I bring you my thanks, O Lord, for the simple joys of this
day —
    for the beauty of trees and gardens;
    for the trust of those about me;
    for things to do, and strength to do them.
Some things I fully meant to do, I have not done. Forgive me.
Some people I meant to get in touch with, I have forgotten.
Forgive me.
Some words I have spoken would have been better unsaid.
Forgive me.
    So bring me to the end of the day aware of your mercy;
    aware of your everlasting keeping and patience;
    trusting in what I know of your attitude to me, through
                Christ, my Lord.
Strengthen the great company of believers in the world,
which is your Church. Bless and guide all who worship you
this night, all who serve you with gifts of heart and hand; all
missionaries far from their own folk; all translators and distributors of the Scriptures. We are all your children; gather us
in, O Father, and give us your peace.   AMEN

Daily Reading

The law of the Lord is perfect, reviving the soul; the testi-
    mony of the Lord is sure, making wise the simple;
the precepts of the Lord are right, rejoicing the heart; the
    commandment of the Lord is pure; enlightening the eyes;
the fear of the Lord is clean, enduring for ever; the ordinances
    of the Lord are true, and righteous altogether.
More to be desired are they than gold, even much fine gold;
    sweeter also than honey and drippings of the honeycomb.
Moreover by them is thy servant warned; in keeping them
    there is great reward.   Psalm 19:7-11

SEVENTH DAY

In the Morning

O God, whose fatherly nature I partly know, and partly do not
know, I come to you because Jesus has encouraged me to do
so.

I praise you for what I have learned through the words of
the prophets, the praise and prayers of the psalmists, the words
of the apostles.

I am enriched by the lives of many good and courageous
people – and by their witness to your supporting love and care.

I claim that same love and care today –

for myself, and all who make up my family;

for friends and acquaintances close to me;

for those whose own trust is unsure, unsteady.

I bring you my thanks for the enriching experiences and
thoughts –

that have come to me through preachers and teachers;

that have come to me through hospitality;

that have come to me through travel abroad, and books at
home;

that have come through the gladsome and deeply moving
gift of music and song.

O God, I am ashamed that sometimes I have taken these good
things of right –

forgive me that I have held close things to be shared;

forgive me that ever I have put things before people;

forgive me that ever I have forgotten that I am an immortal
spirit;

forgive me that ever I have allowed this world's interests
to count for too much.

Let my faith be proven as lively in action today, as it is in
speech.   AMEN

SEVENTH DAY

In the Evening

As I come to my rest at day's end, O God, let it be with praise
upon my lips. As I take time to look back over this day past,
let me show humility. As I recollect those whose lives have
touched mine, let me give thanks. O God, who has parted the
daylight from the dark, and made to rejoice all

> growing things of park and countryside;
>
> developing human personalities;
>
> creative gifts of artists, musicians, writers;
>
> administrative concern of mayors and councils,

show us how to live well together in your world. Let the gifts
entrusted to each, bless us all. Let old feuds die, and faults be
forgotten, that the past hide us not from the things of justice
and love and truth that belong to the days ahead. Help me to
take my own full share in the life of my community. For
Christ's sake.   AMEN

Daily Reading

Paul said: 'If there is any encouragement in Christ, any incen-
tive of love, any participation in the Spirit, any affection and
sympathy, complete my joy by being of the same mind, having
the same love, being in full accord and of one mind. Do
nothing from selfishness or conceit, but in humility count
others better than yourselves. Let each of you look not only to
his own interests, but also to the interests of others. Have this
mind among yourselves, which is yours in Christ Jesus, who,
though he was in the form of God, did not count equality
with God a thing to be grasped, but emptied himself, taking
the form of a servant, being born in the likeness of men.'

Philippians 2 :1-7

EIGHTH DAY

In the Morning

Make me aware of your nearness, O God, this day – I do not ask that you will be near – only that I may be aware. You are always near. In every age, men and women have hushed their hearts at the day's beginning, to recollect your holy promises, and to surrender themselves anew. Life has been long on this earth, and many have left us pictures, poems, songs and writings, to enrich us as we follow on.

Into your loving keeping, I commend this day – all dear to me; all tied by bonds of relationship, by service, by shared responsibility.

Give me gentleness with the very young, and the very old; give me respect for the views of others removed from my own;

give me generosity in the use of my money and possessions.

O God, you have entrusted me with a variety of good things – let me use them well, and to your lasting glory. You have fashioned my heart to seek you, my will to do your will in the earth this day, my heart to warm with love toward you.

If sorrow comes this day, enable me to meet it with steady eyes – knowing that whatever comes, nothing can prove you inadequate;

If new truth comes this day, through the spoken or read word, loosen my prejudices that it may find a lodging-place in my mind;

If success crowns my long-sustained effort this day, let me accept it with thanksgiving, and with a suitable humility.

I give you thanks for the security of home-life;

for the ties which bind men and women through the years;

for experiences shared with trust, for burdens borne with courage.

Let no word or action of mine make it harder for another, or any mannerism jar a sensitive spirit. Keep me considerate and kind, for Christ's sake.   AMEN

EIGHTH DAY

In the Evening

Eternal Father, ever gracious, I bow my head in your holy presence without fear. I speak the secret things of my heart and mind that I do not readily uncover to others. I wait for your free forgiveness, and assurance of strength to overcome temptations which have faulted me today.

Forgive me for casualness – many a bush has flamed beside the way and, unlike Moses at his shepherding, I have not been aware of your nearness, nor taken the shoes from off my feet in worship.

Forgive me for lack of praise – that great deeds of kindness and comforting support have impinged on my day, and unlike the Psalmist, I have not raised my voice in praise and thanksgiving.

Forgive me for the poorness of my discipleship – that unlike Peter and John and their colleagues, I have grown calculating in my giving, and limited in my witness to your love.

For Christ's sake, I ask these blessings.   AMEN

Daily Reading

Now Moses was keeping the flock of his father-in-law, Jethro, the priest of Midian; and he led his flock to the west side of the wilderness, and came to Horeb, the mountain of God. And the angel of the Lord appeared to him in a flame of fire out of the midst of a bush; and he looked, and lo, the bush was burning, yet it was not consumed. And Moses said, 'I will turn aside and see this great sight, why the bush is not burnt.' When the Lord saw that he turned aside to see, God called to him out of the bush, 'Moses, Moses!' And he said, 'Here am I.' Then he said, 'Do not come near; put off your shoes from your feet, for the place on which you are standing is holy ground.'

Exodus 3:1-5

NINTH DAY

In the Morning

O God, creator of all good, light streams into my room, and
the new day is here. I do not know what it holds of your
mercy, and sustaining providence. Strengthen my faith this
day; save me from vague goodwill that evades real situa-
tions —
    that excuses me from concern for others;
    that results in idle hands;
    that spells for me self-pity.
As I go about my affairs, let me recognize the difference
    between loneliness and solitude;
    loneliness the pain of being alone;
    solitude the glory of being alone.
I give you thanks for the blessings of memory, that gather
in riches
    from those who grew up with me;
    from the books and songs I love;
    from the lovely sights I have seen.
I rejoice in the links I have with the big world of men and
women
    through friends and visitors;
    through travel and reading;
    through journals and newspapers, radio and TV.
Though often the news of the day distresses me, let me not
forget that
    this is your world, and that right and beauty
    and truth will be triumphant in the end,
    because you are the Lord God who reigns for ever.   AMEN

NINTH DAY

In the Evening

O Lord of life, as the sounds of the busy day drop away, make me more aware of your nearness at a deep level. Receive my praise for the fulness of this day – for its fellowship with friends, in person, by letters, by phone calls;

> for congenial acquaintances, who might well become friends;

> for the interest of strangers who have greeted me courteously.

If my positive contribution to community goodwill this day has been small, forgive me – for over-concern with my own affairs, at others' expense;

> for uninviting tasks shelved, unexciting visits postponed;

> for opportunities of service overlooked, and thus refused.

Let me know the reality of your forgiving love, that I may come to my sleep without distress.

I pray for all with special needs this night – doctors and nurses on duty; pilots and crews flying through space, and all who journey with them; policemen and firemen, about their tasks; railway-men and engine-drivers peering into the darkness; lighthouse keepers and their families; captains of ships, and all who go down to the sea in ships. Keep them all secure and alert.   AMEN

Daily Reading

Paul said: None of us lives to himself, and none of us dies to himself. If we live, we live to the Lord; and if we die, we die to the Lord; so then, whether we live or whether we die, we are the Lord's. For to this end Christ died and lived again, that he might be Lord both of the dead and of the living.

Why do you pass judgement on your brother? Or you, why do you despise your brother? For we shall all stand before the judgement seat of God; for it is written, 'As I live, says the Lord, every knee shall bow to me, and every tongue shall give praise to God.'

So each of us shall give account of himself to God.

Romans 14:7-12

TENTH DAY

In the Morning

O God, in whose fatherly hands are the issues of life and
death, light and darkness are in your keeping –
    let me face this new day with eagerness and hope;
    let my standard of values today be those of your Kingdom;
    let my serious affairs be lightened with laughter and fun.
I give you thanks for the dependence of little children;
    for the companionship and challenge of youth;
    for the knowledge and responsibility of maturity;
    for the remembered experiences of old age.
Let the gift of love be mine to share generously this day –
    with all who face solitary lives, or lonely;
    with all whose strength is no match for their tasks;
    with all whose retirement is at hand, and unwelcome.
I praise you for the beauty of the changing seasons, the colours,
and shapes;
    and all the energies of renewal known to nature;
    all the many forms of beauty and colour before my eyes;
    all the diverse forms of animal and bird life, each so fas-
        cinating, so beautifully created.
O God, in whom we all live and move and have our being,
whether we recognize you or not,
    let us walk humbly today beneath your sky;
    let us give thanks for the very breath we breathe, for life;
    let us know no separation between things sacred and
        secular – all yours.
In the name of Jesus Christ who made such a wonderful thing
of life in this world.   AMEN

TENTH DAY

In the Evening

As day draws in, and soft lights merge into darkness, I seek reassurance of your love and keeping. You have not made me sufficient in myself; you have set within me a hunger for realities beyond this ever-present world.

Forgive me for thoughts and actions this day which have slurred over the sharp, clear edges of reality; that have found me thoughtless and slack.

I have met some new experiences today, some new people, some new ideas — keep my heart and mind open to all that is beautiful and good and true.

Bless my dear friends afar, whom now I see but seldom — keep them, I pray; strengthen and guide any of them making difficult decisions, about family affairs.

Bless all who are nearing the time when they must cease living alone, and seek some other life-style; all who have become frail in body, unable to deal with the physical challenges of home and garden.

Bless all involved in the building and administration of homes and villages of peace and security for the aged. Especially bless matrons and their staffs, that the real spirit of home may dwell in their midst.

So bless us all, according to our many needs, in the name of Christ, our Lord.   AMEN

Daily Reading

The fruit of the Spirit is love, peace, patience, kindness, goodness, faithfulness, gentleness, self-control; against such there is no law. And those who belong to Christ Jesus have crucified the flesh with its passions and desires.

If we live by the Spirit, let us also walk by the Spirit. Let us have no self-conceit, no provoking of one another, no envy of one another.   Galatians 5 :22-26

ELEVENTH DAY

In the Morning

O Lord, it is astonishing how the days pass, the dates pile up;
you know what it is in my heart to do today. Let it be done
with your blessing, and become part of your Kingdom on
earth. Let the values that Jesus set at the centre of his life,
be my values – his graciousness be mine, his perseverance; his
outreaching friendliness. I rejoice in what I know of his life,
through the gospels, through fine preachers and teachers and
books and pictures.

Hold in your keeping today any who are unsure, any who
are setting about a fresh undertaking, any whose shyness is a
disadvantage.

Hold in your keeping young couples setting up new homes,
any entering into the responsibilities and delights of parenthood.

Hold in your keeping any who have succumbed to selfishness, all who have become cynical, and faithless.

O God, there is no lovely thing but comes to us from you
– let none of us handle today these holy gifts irresponsibly,
selfishly, casually.

Keep me from flattery today;

Keep me from setting myself above others;

Keep me from uncreative criticism;

Keep me from lowering my standards.

O God, give me the courage I need to forget my hurts,
to add some note of appreciation where another's struggles
are known; to share any new thought, any new incident, any
new joke that will lighten a dark sky for another.

You know all who are especially in my thoughts just now
—— and —— these are dear to me, but infinitely more dear
to you, I know. Guide us all in our choices this day, in all our
undertakings, all our associations.   AMEN

In the Evening

In this quietness, O Lord, I would drop my haste, and listen;
    I would shed my pride and wait humbly;
    I would confess my sins, and await forgiveness.
    I am a member of your Church in all the world, a servant
of your purpose in
    things sacred and secular – all one;
    a pilgrim after truth and loveliness.
Bless all who have crossed my threshold this day, all who
have phoned me,
    all who have written,
    all who have prayed for me, as I now pray for them.
Grant us all your peace which passeth all understanding.

AMEN

Daily Reading

Wash yourselves; make yourselves clean;
remove the evil of your doings from before my eyes;
cease to do evil, learn to do good;
seek justice, correct oppression;
defend the fatherless, plead for the widow.

'Come now, let us reason together, says the Lord:
though your sins are like scarlet,
they shall be as white as snow;
though they are red like crimson,
they shall become like wool.'

Isaiah 1 : 16-18

31

TWELFTH DAY

In the Morning

O God, I marvel that no two mornings are exactly alike —
that your creative gifts have such variety —
    bless all my meetings with others today;
    bless all my speech with others today;
    bless any service I can render others today.
It is strengthening to know that Jesus wakened to life day
by day, in this world — that he gave thanks, as I give thanks,
for life;
    that he had need of food and clothing;
    that he mingled with neighbours;
    that he worked the hours round at an honourable trade.
Bless, in his name, all who bend over work-benches today;
all who move amongst fellow-workers — that good things and
true may result.
    Guide all who work with their minds and imaginations;
    guide all who work with their hands, with machines;
    guide all disabled and unfit for any chosen service.
Let each serve in your sight alone, as faithfully as if all the
world saw. For the sake of Christ the true workman.   AMEN

In the Evening

Heavenly Father, to you I brought my first thoughts on waking — I bring you now my last thoughts before sleeping; and
they are thoughts of your goodness, this day. You have brought
me safely through its hours, you have given me food and
clothing sufficient; you have given me work to do, and strength
and ability to do it. You have surrounded me with beautiful
things — trees, hills, rivers and cornlands; you have given me

the companionship of animals and birds; you have entrusted to me this part of your dumb creation.

I give thanks for beautiful and helpful things of man's creation — houses and churches and bridges and streets and lanes; for lovely fabrics for garments and furnishings, for leathers and metals and plastics; let me use these things well. I give thanks for shapes and colours which please my eyes and my touch. I give thanks for books and pictures; I give thanks for music and song; for crafts and artistic possessions. Not one hour has come and gone without the imprint of your love upon it.

Bless especially, during the darkness, any who suffer; any who know grief; any who face death; any who are involved in the anguish of accident and hurt.

Bless especially, during the darkness, any who travel by road, sea or air; that they may do it alertly, responsibly. In the name of Christ our Lord who walked this earth.   AMEN

Daily Reading

Paul said: I bow my knees before the Father, from whom every family in heaven and on earth is named, that according to the riches of his glory he may grant you to be strengthened with might through his Spirit in the inner man, and that Christ may dwell in your hearts through faith; that you, being rooted and grounded in love, may have power to comprehend with all the saints what is the breadth and length and height and depth, and to know the love of Christ which surpasses knowledge, that you may be filled with all the fulness of God.

Ephesians 3 : 14-19

In the Morning

O Lord, I rejoice to waken assured of your keeping this day
— that in work or leisure, in health or sickness, in joy or
sorrow, I am kept in love. Let me never take these good gifts
for granted, or receive them without loving acknowledgement.
  Bless me as I go about the routine tasks of this day;
  bless me as I plan new things to do — and do them;
  bless me as my work touches other lives close by.
Deliver me from self-importance; grant me a humble spirit,
ready to learn and to do. Keep the edges of my mind clean,
my imagination fresh and beautiful; let me use my body well,
to your honour and glory only. Let my mind reach out into
wider knowledge.
  Give me peace and serenity as I face what the day holds;
  give me relaxation and naturalness in my manner;
  give me joyfulness and kindliness.
I am not worthy of the least of your mercies, but you have
not made your good to me to depend on my worth; you have
given me the experience of childhood and youth, the growing
realizations of adulthood and maturity; let me give back to
you in thanksgiving, what gifts I can bring.
  So enrich my comings and goings in your world;
  so enable me to live as a whole person, a glad person;
  so bring me in at nightfall, unashamed, offering something
  worthwhile this day.   AMEN

In the Evening

In the quiet of this place apart, I take time for recollection.
Without assurance of your forgiveness and restoration, I
would know no peace at day's end; without what I know of

you through Jesus Christ, I would have no confidence to pray. Jesus taught me to call you Father, and to depend on your character as he knew it, and revealed it. And this I do, in my own way, here and now. I ask your forgiveness for anything unworthy that I have done or thought this day – for anything I ought to have done, and failed to do. I ask your keeping through the hours of darkness, of unconsciousness. And what I pray for myself, I pray for others especially dear to me – for —— and —— and —— Distance can make no difference to you.

Some things I promised to do this day have been overlooked; some people I meant to pop in and see must wait till tomorrow; the day has become more full than ever I expected.

Forgive me for anything I have done too hurriedly, too carelessly, to own before your eyes. In the name of Jesus, my Saviour. AMEN

Daily Reading

Who is a God like thee, pardoning iniquity
   and passing over transgression
   for the remnant of his inheritance?
He does not retain his anger for ever
   because he delights in steadfast love.
He will again have compassion upon us,
   he will tread our iniquities under foot.
Thou wilt cast all our sins
   into the depths of the sea.

Micah 7:18-19

FOURTEENTH DAY

In the Morning

O Lord, the light that reaches my eyes this morning, is your light; the air that I breathe is your air; in your wholeness I live and move and have my being. Though well, and eager, I am not sufficient in myself – I cannot meet the possible delights or dangers of this day alone.

Make yourself known to those who face this new day without remembering these essentials; all who grab at gains for their own ends; all who push others aside, in getting their rewards. Through someone, show them a better way of life today.

And take hold of my own standards, and enrich them;
take hold of my hands, and use them well;
take hold of my words, and keep them truthful and kind.

Deliver me from boastfulness; from unhelpful criticism; from lack of sympathy; from harshness in my relationships, especially with the young, the unsure, the lonely, the aged.
Bless and hold today
all who find themselves in hospital;
all who find themselves in court;
all who find themselves in prison.

We are your children – foolish often in our choices; selfish often in our plans; inexperienced often when we confront a difficulty; unyielding often in our prejudices; unkind often in our judgements. Forgive us, and show us how to mend our ways. Give us patience to keep trying, as we mingle with others, and so enrich life for us all. AMEN

FOURTEENTH DAY

In the Evening

O God, you know what has been packed into this full day —
from the moment I opened my eyes this morning. Now as I go
over it all, tiredness creeps over my body, my mind, my spirit.
So my prayer is brief — though sincere. Keep me when I cannot
keep myself, and bring me to a new day, as eager as I wakened
this morning. I have this confidence in your keeping love,
through Christ, who knew tiredness too, and slept on a pillow
in the stern of a boat.   AMEN

Daily Reading

Now a certain man was ill, Lazarus of Bethany, the village of
Mary and her sister Martha. It was Mary who anointed the
Lord with ointment and wiped his feet with her hair, whose
brother Lazarus was ill. So the sisters sent to him, saying,
'Lord, he whom you love is ill.' But when Jesus heard it he
said, 'This illness is not unto death; it is for the glory of God,
so that the Son of God may be glorified by means of it.' . . .
Martha said to him, 'I know that he will rise again in the
resurrection at the last day.' Jesus said to her, 'I am the
resurrection and the life; he who believes in me, though he
die, yet shall he live, and whoever lives and believes in me
shall never die. Do you believe this?' She said to him, 'Yes,
Lord! I believe that you are the Christ, the Son of God, he who
is coming into the world.'

When she had said this, she went and called her sister
Mary, saying quietly, 'The Teacher is here and is calling for
you.' And when she heard it, she rose quickly and went to
him.   John 11:1-4, 24-29

FIFTEENTH DAY

In the Morning

O God, I open my eyes again in your lovely world. The things of the countryside, mountains, hills, lakes, and streams speak your praise — and with greater powers, I speak your praise, too —

    I praise you for the power that keeps me when asleep;
    I praise you for my consciousness returned;
    I praise you for my human faculties stirring.

Surround with your keeping this day all with whom I share life — our needs vary; our plans vary; our choices; our personalities — we like different things, and dislike different things.

    Strengthen our friendships beyond our home circle today —
    Take special care of those who are worried ——
    Take care of all those who are thoughtless, reckless ——

So bless us in our goings out, and our comings in, that we may live at all times answerable to you, and dependent on you. Let us interpret love, faith and hope in our affairs this day.

    I am supported by the many fine people I know;
    I give thanks for the courage of so many;
    I praise you that you have given laughter and fun to help us on our way.   AMEN

In the Evening

As the coolness and quiet of night rests on all about me now, restore those who are tired with routine tasks of home-making, nursing, teaching, engaging in commerce, in government; and unravel social problems for those exhausted with dealing with those who have fallen beside the way. You know the needs of each, in a way that I cannot possibly do. So often I pray poorly, because I understand imperfectly.

Keep this night all who must work whilst others of us sleep – hospital staffs, caretakers, keepers of law and order, engine-drivers and guards, pilots of planes and crews, captains of ships and all who go down to the sea, keepers of all-night cafeterias, petrol pumps, and suchlike services.

And when the new day comes, let not the mistakes and follies of any of us hold us back from a new beginning. Keep us all humble, and true to the highest of our secret aspirations, for Christ's sake.   AMEN

Daily Reading

O God, thou art my God. I seek thee,
   my soul thirsts for thee; my flesh faints for thee,
as in a dry and weary land where no water is.
So I have looked upon thee in the sanctuary,
   beholding thy power and glory.
Because thy steadfast love is better than life,
   my lips will praise thee.
So I will bless thee as long as I live;
I will lift up my hands and call on thy name.

My soul is feasted as with marrow and fat,
   and my mouth praises thee with joyful lips,
when I think of thee upon my bed,
   and meditate on thee in the watches of the night;
for thou hast been my help,
   and in the shadow of thy wings I sing for joy.
My soul clings to thee; thy right hand upholds me.

                                                       Psalm 63 : 1-8

SIXTEENTH DAY

In the Morning

O God, it seems no time since I shut my eyes – and now the new day is here. Let it prove a good one in my home, and sphere of service, and in all my personal relationships.

    You know those whose names are in my mind at once —— and ——

    those whose special needs just now are known to me ——

    those estranged from some with whom they are rightfully linked —— and ——

O God, grant wisdom and loving patience today, to all who tend-old people who are demanding; who are ill; who are slow in movement; in sight or hearing. All who continue responsibilities in the home when others have married and gone ——

    Bless their services to those who are mentally frail;

    to those who are bedfast; those whose days here are numbered;

    to those who look into the future with fear.

O God, grant eagerness to all who tend gardens this day, matching labour to the seasons, and soils, bringing forth beauty and fragrance for all; tidying up ugly corners, bringing order out of chaos; placing seats where the elderly and frail may rest; planting trees for the days ahead.

    Bless also those whose creative skills add meaning and colour to our homes – artists, potters, weavers, authors of our books;

    all who enrich the community – sculptors, dramatists;

    all who speak through sermon, address, and poetry-reading.

Your great creative purposes continue in the world you have made –

    It is wonderful to have a share in them today;

    let the gifts of my mind and my hands be shared gladly;

    let my spirit add graciousness and joy today.   AMEN

SIXTEENTH DAY

In the Evening

O Lord of life in its infinite variety, I thank you for what this day has brought of interest, and delight – for its activities, and now when my energies are expended, the gift of relaxation and rest.

You are the God of night, as of day, of doing, and ceasing to do.

Help me to use well the quiet that you have given me just now – that I may be saved from ingratitude, and from a false sense of achievement. Let me bring all that I have, and all that I have done this day, to the scrutiny of your loving presence. May there be something of worth in my service that will be acceptable, and useful in your Kingdom eternal.   AMEN

Daily Reading

Now as they went on their way, he entered a village; and a woman named Martha received him into her house. And she had a sister called Mary, who sat at the Lord's feet and listened to his teaching. But Martha was distracted with much serving; and she went to him and said, 'Lord, do you not care that my sister has left me to serve all alone? Tell her then to help me.' But the Lord answered her, 'Martha, Martha, you are anxious and troubled about many things; one thing is needful. Mary has chosen the good portion, which shall not be taken away from her.'   Luke 10 :38-42

SEVENTEENTH DAY

In the Morning

Gracious Lord, my thoughts move out into the wider world, as I waken in this peaceful place. I remember the many who face this day, unrested; hungry; poorly clad; bewildered; sick; homeless.

I pray for all who give service abroad;

I pray for the world's peace-makers;

I pray for all who seek justice and labour for it.

Bless all who work with little children in poor countries; all who give medical and nursing aid; all who help to build relationships of hope and dignity and worth.

I pray that those who have skills may share them;

I pray that those who have money will give it;

I pray that to young people may come the challenge of building a better world.

Bless those who tour alone or with parties, in an effort to see something of the way of the world beyond their own shores; save them from superficiality, from superiority of country, colour, or clime.

Bring us closer to each other as human beings;

Set us to think how life comes daily to others;

Let not our sympathies be dispersed, or swamped in sentimentality.

We pray for those who translate the Scriptures into the world's tongues, that the gospel of Christ may be shared by all; that the darkness of sin, and fear, and idolatry may gradually be done away with.

Many who serve your Kingdom in international spheres are known to me by name —— and —— Keep them in their particular setting today. In Christ's name. AMEN

SEVENTEENTH DAY

In the Evening

Gracious Father, I bring my thanks for the new things I have learned this day; for the new things I have done; for the new people I have met.

Thank you for people ready to share what they know;
Thank you for people ready to share what they have;
Thank you for people ready to share what they are in the deeps of personality.

I rejoice that you have not made us to travel alone, but to know the enrichment of sharing in this life as we go; help us more and more to do this generously and gladly, in the name of Christ.   AMEN

Daily Reading

But where shall wisdom be found?
    And where is the place of understanding?
Man does not know the way to it,
    and it is not found in the land of the living.
The deep says, 'It is not in me,'
    And the sea says, 'It is not with me.'
It cannot be gotten for gold,
    and silver cannot be weighed as its price.
It cannot be valued in the gold of Ophir,
    in precious onyx or sapphire.
Gold and glass cannot equal it,
    nor can it be exchanged for jewels of fine gold . . .
Behold, the fear of the Lord, that is wisdom.

                                                    Job 28 :12-17, 28

EIGHTEENTH DAY

In the Morning

O Lord of life, direct and keep me this day — clear my vision, keep my step light, and my heart loyal and true. And what I ask for myself with my first breath, I ask for those whom I love.

Guard especially today
  all whose work is dangerous;
  all whose work is tedious;
  all whose work is lonely.

Guard especially today all whose work is with people;
  let them show a proper respect;
  let them try always to understand;
  let them put people before things.

Guard today all who travel
  by the busy roads of our land;
  by the sea — in small boats and ships;
  by foot, about the city pavements.

All who have special needs of other kinds, I commit to you—
  any involved in accidents this day;
  any held captive by drugs;
  any overborne by a sense of shame.

I am thinking especially of —— and —— and ——
  I am glad that each is known to you;
  that each is loved by you;
  that you have power to do the wisest things to help them.

Bless all our goings out, and our comings in, this day, O Lord.

AMEN

EIGHTEENTH DAY

In the Evening

Forgive me, O God, my Father, if I blunder into your presence without reverence or proper readiness of mind and heart. I take so much for granted; I move from one task to another with such haste; I fall back on words so easily; I bring forth deeds of love so tardily. Forgive me. And as I wait in your presence, let me know that nothing lies in between our forgiving, loving relationship.

I bless you for all who have served your Kingdom this day, without thought of reward; all who have shown compassion for those in need; for all who have overcome temptation, in your strength. Prepare us all to start again tomorrow.

Watch by little children as they sleep, tucked-in lovingly; watch by the sick as they lie wakeful; watch by the worried, as they toss and turn over their problems; watch over those whose earthly life is ebbing – deliver them from all fear, strengthen their trustful relationships with your loving self. This, I ask, knowing well my own limitations to help. For the sake of Jesus, who gave me confidence to pray.　　AMEN

Daily Reading

Jesus said : 'If a man does not abide in me, he is cast forth as a branch and withers; and the branches are gathered, thrown into the fire and burned. If you abide in me, and my words abide in you, ask whatever you will, and it shall be done for you. By this my Father is glorified, that you bear much fruit, and so prove to be my disciples. As the Father has loved me, so have I loved you; abide in my love. If you keep my commandments, you will abide in my love, just as I have kept my Father's commandments and abide in his love. These things I have spoken to you, that my joy may be in you, and that your joy may be full.'　　John 15 :6-11

NINETEENTH DAY

In the Morning

O Lord, this is another wonderful morning – a new beginning, an unguessed opportunity to be and do. Let me make good use of it – using my refreshed body and mind; exercising my best thought in preparation for service; showing gentle patience with people and things.

Save me from taking myself too seriously, too ponderously – let laughter have a place in my day; let my imagination have room to introduce me to beauty and joy; let my hands display their competence and delight in creation.

Guide my relationships with others about me today – those whom I know and trust; those whom I do not know; those whom I suspect of selfish aims; those with whom I seem to have little or nothing in common.

Bless all who look to me for friendship and help in any way – especially the very young, the disabled, the very old, the anxious, the incompetent, the discouraged.

I rejoice that no surprise can reach me without your knowledge – and your power to make of it something worthwhile, something patterned into a rich experience.

I rejoice in the energies of youth, the wisdom of middle age, the memories of old age. Teach us how to live together; teach us the living principles of Jesus Christ, who in a setting so different, lived and died and rose again triumphant. In his name, I fashion this prayer.   AMEN

In the Evening

When the day ends, and darkness gathers round, men and women have always turned to you, O God. Beside strange altars they have made their prayers, in strange languages they have expressed their petitions.

But nothing in all your creation is strange to you – no human need is unknown, no earnest prayer unheard. Our needs as the day ends are as varied as our own days spent, our personalities. These you know.

Forgive those of us who are headstrong and foolish; those of us simple and ignorant; those of us shy and hesitant; those of us slow and literal. When we see what is to be done, let us move into responsible action.

I remember in your presence this night —— and —— and ——

I give thanks for the friendship of —— and —— and ——

I find encouragement in the help of —— and —— and —— and ——

Keep me safe whilst I sleep, O Lord,
bring me to the new day, ready to try again,
more trustful in your guidance than up till now.

To your honour and glory.   AMEN

Daily Reading

Preserve me, O God, for in thee I take refuge.
 I say to the Lord, 'Thou art my Lord;
 I have no good apart from thee.'
As for the saints in the land, they are the noble,
 in whom is all my delight.
Those who choose another god multiply their sorrows;
 their libations of blood I will not pour out
 or take their names upon my lips.
The Lord is my chosen portion and my cup;
 thou holdest my lot.
The lines have fallen for me in pleasant places;
 yea, I have a goodly heritage.

                                        Psalm 16:1-6

TWENTIETH DAY

In the Morning

As I rise to face the new day, let me wash and dress with pleasure, and plan out my work with eagerness and interest.

I shall meet many people today, before night gathers us all in again for sleep – I shall turn my hands to a great variety of tasks.

Whatever calls for my attention today, cannot be outside your interest; sacred or secular, cannot be outside the scope of your blessing.

It gives me joy to remember the little home in Nazareth, where Mary and Joseph lived and served; where a family grew and shared life.

It pleases my senses to be surrounded by growing things – grass and garden, wild creatures, pets and birds. For the lovely variety of life, I bless you.

Guide today all upon whom rest responsibilities of choice –
    members of committees and boards and councils;
    makers of rules that affect others' lives;
    moulders of public opinion and action.

Guide today all ministers, priests, deaconesses and nuns;
    all who live and serve in community;
    all set to serve in lonely places of the earth;
    all nearing the close of their working years.

Enable us all during the hours of today
    to establish a love of beauty, where is drabness;
    to replace disappointment with hope;
    to exchange generosity for meanness.

AMEN

TWENTIETH DAY

In the Evening

You know, O God, my Father, those who are most in my
mind as I come to this period of rest and recollection ——
and —— and ——

I am not wise enough to do for them all that they need; I
am not strong enough to meet all their problems and resolve
them – so I bring them to you.

Let me not fail in my obligations to them – in my thoughts,
my judgements, my loving concern.

If there is friction, let me bring to the situation the cool
balm of understanding, and long-time patience.

If there is pretence, let me do my share to foster straight-
forwardness and confidence, that living truth may prevail.

If I have failed in any of these essentials today, forgive me.

If I have been over-hasty and thoughtless today, forgive me.

If I have been too ready to reckon myself right always, forgive me and renew my attitudes.

So bring wholeness out of foolishness and hurt; joy out of
grief; love out of selfishness and self-righteousness.   AMEN

Daily Reading

Paul said : 'I appeal to you therefore, brethren, by the mercies
of God, to present your bodies as a living sacrifice, holy and
acceptable to God, which is your spiritual worship. Do not be
conformed to this world but be transformed by the renewal of
your mind, that you may prove what is the will of God, what
is good and acceptable and perfect. For by the grace given to
me I bid every one among you not to think of himself more
highly than he ought to think.'   Romans 12 : 1-3

In the Morning

O God, I would use my earliest conscious thought for praise!
  to praise you for the new day – your gift;
  to praise you for renewed strength – your gift;
  to praise you for this home in which I waken – your gift.
Take hold of each of my faculties this day, and use them to
your glory.
  Let my work be done with eagerness and satisfaction;
  let my thoughts be above self-gain;
  let my spirit respond to the impress of your love, O Lord.
If I am privileged to open my door to friends, neighbours,
newcomers today –
  Let me use my home and my treasured things happily;
  let me know the secret of setting others at ease;
  let my hospitality from end to end, be to your honour and
    glory.
Hold in your safe-keeping this day, the several members of my
  family —— here —— there —— in another place ——
  This world is large, and full of fascination; hold us all.
  This world is full of opportunities for service; guide us.
  This world is your world, and nothing can separate us from
    your love, in Jesus Christ.
Enable us to face whatever the day brings, confident and full
of courage;
  courteous in our relationships with others;
  joyous in our service, unmindful of self;
  combining our deepest faith with essential action, as natur-
    ally as Christ was able to do.   AMEN

In the Evening

O God, I bring to you my failures, and my successes, this night. Forgive me that, at any time, I have tried to take action alone – I am not adequate for this, experience has now taught me. Forgive me my conceit; and make me from now on more dependent upon your love and strength.

Forgive me if my temper has been roused this day, to another's undoing; if my patience has been short; if my readiness to praise you for all my mercies has been lax. I am very forgetful, very self-assured. Forgive me, I pray. Give me the rest I need this night, and with the new day set me to tasks anew.

I need your clear discernment in the tangle of choices which each day brings; I need your faithfulness in the fulfilment of things undertaken in good spirit; I need your everlasting consideration in relation to others. These lovely qualities you have shown me in Christ, as he lived his life on this earth. So I do not despair. My trust is in your power to make of my life here something beautiful, too.   AMEN

Daily Reading

He shall not judge by what his eyes see,
    or decide by what his ears hear:
but with righteousness he shall judge the poor,
    and decide with equity for the meek of the earth;
and he shall smite the earth with the rod
    of his mouth,
and with the breath of his lips he shall slay
    the wicked.
Righteousness shall be the girdle of his waist,
and faithfulness the girdle of his loins.

                                        Isaiah 11:3-5

TWENTY-SECOND DAY

In the Morning

O Lord, I dedicate anew all my faculties – let me use them
well today.

Control my tongue, that it will not sharpen to unkindly
speech;

control my ears, that they may gather no gossip;

control my sense of touch, that it may be gentle and considerate.

O Lord, bless all whose lives touch mine – those within my
home; those out in the larger community; those in the great
world. Bless those who make it possible for us to exchange
news, receive letters, phone calls, and brief visits for an
exchange of interests.

O Lord, bless all for whom this is a sad anniversary; all
widows and widowers; all far from their homeland; all without congenial companionship; all who struggle with a language not their own.

O Lord, bless those who must spend this day in ugly surroundings – enable them to see how things might be im-
proved, and to do something to realize that need. Bless the
gardens they make, the green things they plant.

O Lord, bless all whose first thoughts are for others –
social-workers, ministers, priests, doctors, nurses, ambulance-
men, firemen, family counsellors, psychiatrists.

Bless all who write today the books and articles that people
will read – keep the edges of their interests clean and their
purposes tied to building up life rather than to smart pulling-
down.

Bless all who speak today where people listen – in schools
and colleges, in radio and TV studios, in Parliament, and in
local committees.

Bless all who work to resolve racial tensions, class hate,
family pride, social superiority, and all that hinders justice,
truth and goodness.

Accept today the work that we do, and the secret and shared thoughts that we think, for the building-up of your everlasting Kingdom.   AMEN

In the Evening

O Lord, you know the tangled thoughts that tumble in my tired mind just now.

    I cannot easily think aright about this full day;

    I cannot judge what has been of most account;

    I cannot boast that selfishness has not crept in.

O Lord, forgive me that I am inclined to take for granted the services

    of those close to me in my home;

    of those in the market-place whom I cannot name;

    of those in the neighbourhood who work to serve us all.

I have been busy about many things today, and now I lie down to sleep. Teach me how to combine the Mary and the Martha spirit, I pray.   AMEN

Daily Reading

Paul wrote of Christ: 'Being found in human form he humbled himself and became obedient unto death, even death on a cross. Therefore God has highly exalted him and bestowed on him the name which is above every name, that at the name of Jesus every knee should bow, in heaven and on earth and under the earth, and every tongue confess that Jesus Christ is Lord, to the glory of God the Father.'

Philippians 2:8-11

In the Morning

O Lord, I bless you for the power to rise from my bed, and
go about my affairs today. I pray for all bedfast, in home and
hospital; and all who tend them. Give to all involved cheerful
patience, genuine knowledge and compassion—
  let pillows give supporting ease;
  let windows admit light and air;
  let the benison of hot water be to hand;
  let books and papers and pictures play their part.
We give you praise for all the miracles of medical science—
  for the devotion of scientists;
  for the generous whose money is put to good use;
  for those who translate into action, new skills;
  for friends and family-members who visit with cheerful
    talk and flowers.
Bless those newly in hospital, who find things strange—
  any shy about their bodies;
  all who minister to them professionally;
  all at home who wonder about them, hourly;
  and all companions of better times, better days.
Stir rich memories during the loneliness of long hours, of
lovely things and happy occasions; call to mind poems and
books and pictures they love, and the visits and longer journeys
shared with others.   AMEN

TWENTY-THIRD DAY

In the Evening

O God, there are many things in each day beyond my power to achieve, or my capacity to understand. Let me live by the things I deeply know, the truths I have discovered real; the certainties of my faith.

Renew in me in this hour of recollection, the spirit of thanksgiving, that no good thing and true which has been part of today may be forgotten; no humble service unacknowledged, in the spirit of my courteous Lord.

You have surrounded me with love far beyond my deserts, raise my heart to praise you sincerely and deeply, I pray, now and for ever.   AMEN

Daily Reading

Open to me the gates of righteousness,
    that I may enter through them
    and give thanks to the Lord.
This is the gate of the Lord;
    the righteous shall enter through it.
I thank thee that thou hast answered me
    and hast become my salvation.
The stone which the builders rejected
    has become the head of the corner.
This is the Lord's doing;
    it is marvellous in our eyes.
This is the day which the Lord has made;
    let us rejoice and be glad in it.

Psalm 118:19-24

In the Morning

O God in whose merciful hands are the issues of life and
death, I am glad I know you as Father of my spirit – I am
glad I have learned from Jesus Christ what manner of Father
you are –

So I face this day with you, confident and glad;

I set myself to routine tasks as they come;

I open my eyes, and my ears, to reminders of your presence
ever near.

Deliver me today from all that is shoddy and superficial –

let my standards today be of the highest;

let my conversation be truthful and creative;

let my hands be ever ready to help another in need.

I bless you for every opportunity to use new skills, to share
new beauty –

let me choose well the books I read;

let me choose well my radio and TV programmes;

let me not despair at the grimness of the newspaper head-
lines.

Let me build this day, this year, on the assurance that this is
your world – that you are in charge of it;

so let me move out with confidence into this day;

so let me commit to your everlasting keeping, my whole
self.

And what I claim for myself, by faith, I claim for those whom
I love.   AMEN

In the Evening

All manner of thoughts gather in my mind, O God, as I come
to this quiet time. There has been all too little time in which
to think during this busy day – its requirements have been so

constant. But now I can think it over in your presence, and try to see how it looks to you.

There have been blunders, some points of selfishness, some words spoken that might have been better unsaid. Forgive me. Where I have been insensible of others' feelings, hurt has been done. Forgive me. Where I have been too busy to listen to another's troubles, someone has struggled alone. Forgive me. Where I have been prideful, or complacent, service has not been rendered. Forgive me.

Take this day into your hands, O God of mercy, and sift from it anything that is good and true – and let the rest be blown away as chaff.

Let any casual contacts this day which have encouraged others have your blessing and grow; let my capacity to live well be stronger tomorrow, as I waken refreshed, to walk into a new day. The night and the day are both yours, O God, and I am yours. Keep me.   AMEN

Daily Reading

Paul writes : 'First of all, then, I urge that supplications, prayers, intercessions, and thanksgivings be made for all men, for kings and all who are in high positions, that we may lead a quiet and peaceable life, godly and respectful in every way. This is good, and it is acceptable in the sight of God our Saviour, who desires all men to be saved and to come to the knowledge of the truth. For there is one God, and there is one mediator between God and men, the man Christ Jesus, who gave himself as a ransom for all . . . I desire then that in every place the men should pray, lifting holy hands without anger or quarrelling.'   1 Timothy 2 : 1-6a, 8

In the Morning

O God, in whom all life begins — I commit myself to your loving care this new day. I have already experienced enough to persuade me to this. But over and above all this, I am persuaded to trust you utterly, by the words and witness of Jesus Christ, my Lord and Master.

> I praise you for the New Testament which brings him clearly before my mind and heart;
> I praise you for the apostles who first set it in writing; and for all who have treasured it;
> I praise you for good men and women, who have translated it into my own language.

Speak to me daily as I turn over its pages; let me read it with my whole mind as well as my heart and imagination; let me look for guidance as I read; let me humbly submit my faulty standards to the standards of Jesus that I see there; his love for me; his love for ordinary people.

> I praise you for the freshness of this new day; and for all who waken to share it with me;
> I praise you for light and air, and beautiful natural things of grass and garden;
> I praise you for the fun of things, awaiting in unexpected corners, as well as the serious and staid.

Take hold of my body, mind and spirit, and show me how to live well; let others looking on, see in my daily witness of Jesus Christ, something winsome and compelling. Bless all who launch out into new discipleship of Christ. And all who minister to their new faith.

AMEN

TWENTY-FIFTH DAY

In the Evening

Eternal Father, I am weary this night. But the words of my prayer are honest and urgent. I cannot live through any day without you – and I cannot come to peace of mind at the day's end without you. I need to be assured of your nearness at this moment.

I bless you that this day has brought for some wonderful happiness – some have fallen in love; some have entered into new homes; some have entered into the responsibilities and joy of parenthood; some have come to new faith in the living Christ.

Strengthen the ties that hold our hearts together in these good adventures. Support us through good times and ill, through serious things and lightsome. Keep us sensitive to others' need, and thankful for our many blessings.

As the night wraps about all nature, wrap your keeping providence about our lives, and the lives of those we love, this night.   AMEN

Daily Reading

Paul writes : 'I do not cease to give thanks for you, remembering you in my prayers, that the God of our Lord Jesus Christ, the Father of glory, may give you a spirit of wisdom and of revelation in the knowledge of him, having the eyes of your hearts enlightened, that you may know what is the hope to which he has called you, what are the riches of his glorious inheritance in the saints, and what is the immeasurable greatness of his power in us who believe, according to the working of his great might which he accomplished in Christ when he raised him from the dead and made him sit at his right hand in the heavenly places, far above all rule and authority and power and dominion, and above every name that is named.'

Ephesians 1 :16-21

TWENTY-SIXTH DAY

In the Morning

Heavenly Father, I turn my first conscious thoughts towards you –

    in praise for my night's rest in comfort and health;

    in praise for the good fellowship of my home;

    in praise for friends who are so generous towards me.

Be pleased to accept these praises, O Lord, along with those of hosts above –

    along with countless Christians on earth, loving you, serving you;

    along with members of my own congregation here, at this time;

    along with those of the great company speaking praise in tongues unfamiliar to me.

We are all your children – of whatever skin colour, language, or clime –

    hold in your special care this day all set on peace-making;

    hold in your special care this day all who suffer injustice;

    hold in your special care this day the hungry, the hard-pressed for shelter and clothing.

Let those of us who fare well, be ready to share with those who fare ill –

    let no surplus clothing hang in my wardrobe;

    let no uneaten food be cast into my waste-can;

    let me not fall to the temptation to buy things I do not need whilst others want for essentials.

You have created us to live in this plenteous earth as one family – teach us how to care in great ways and small, that none may lie down in hunger, or waken to be haunted by the same. Bless all farmers, fruit-growers, and merchants, all manufacturers and distributors – that the earth's crops and commodities may be fairly shared. Our human resources are not sufficient for our deepest needs – we need your forgiving love, your sustaining grace, your keeping. We rejoice that we have not to persuade you to give us what we need; that you are already more willing to give than we to receive.   AMEN

In the Evening

Have mercy, O Lord, on all who have brought upon themselves and others needless suffering this day, I pray —
   on all who have not thought to pray for themselves;
   on all grown cynical, and forgetful of thy goodness;
   on all seeing in your world no proof of your presence.
No dawn moves on to dusk, and into darkness, without your living thought for those of us whom you have created.

We are insufficient in ourselves; we need your divine providence every hour, your guidance when we come to the crossroads of choice.

And we need the fellowship of others who love you, as we do, worshipping as we do, serving as we do, in your Church in the world.

We find our sufficiency in your gospel of grace — and give thanks.   AMEN

Daily Reading

Then the King will say to those at his right hand, 'Come, O blessed of my Father, inherit the kingdom prepared for you from the foundation of the world; for I was hungry and you gave me food, I was thirsty and you gave me drink, I was a stranger and you welcomed me, I was naked and you clothed me, I was sick and you visited me, I was in prison and you came to me.' Then the righteous will answer him, 'Lord when . . . ?' And the King will answer them, 'Truly, I say to you, as you did it to one of the least of these my brethren, you did it to me.'   Matthew 25:34-37, 40

In the Morning

So soon after I shut my eyes, O Lord, the morning comes —
and I must rise to face a new day.

> Let me hold fast to the things of your Kingdom that I
> believe;
> let me hold fast to past experiences that have revealed you;
> let me hold fast to habits of worship and meditation, for
> your glory, and my enrichment.

I love this world in which you have placed me to live — its
mountains and plains, its rivers and streams, its mighty seas,
and shady pools. I love its colours and shapes, its songs and
dances that express pure joy and happiness.

I love its wild creatures; and most of all its little children,
full of sweet trustfulness; its young folk ready to adventure
far; its considerate and caring people of middle age; its old
people of long memories and small strength now. O Father,
our needs are as varied as our ages, and differing personalities. Some of us are practical people, some have artistic gifts,
some are shy, others of us ready to rise to any challenge. You
know us better than we know ourselves — and you know what
is best for us. Our understanding of our inmost needs is so
small, so faulty, so full of fear.

Enable us today to trust you as never before; to desire
sincerely your will above all our own little secret plans.

So enable us to use our natural gifts, our acquired knowledge, our handy skills. And lift our eyes to horizons beyond
our own limited round. But let us not give ourselves to remote
undertakings, and forget the humble tasks near at hand.

Bless this day all whose work outmatches their physical
strength; all whose eyes weary with seeing; all whose ears
have become dull to music and human speech.

Bless this day all whose contemporaries have moved away,
or died; all whose memories of busier times have grown dim.
Whatever our special need, nothing that we can express in

prayer, comes as a surprise to you. This adds up to joy and confidence to us, here and now. In Christ's name.   AMEN

In the Evening

The darkness wraps me round, O God, and the stars peep out. The noises of the busy day are hushed – and I hush my restless heart in your presence. I rejoice that in your keeping, I am safe, whatever befalls – and that all whom I love, are much more loved by you, and much more wisely and well, than I can love them. I remember especially —— and —— and —— just now.

This has been a good day – and I bring my thanks for its interests. This brief prayer carries the spontaneous thanks of my heart; you know all my secret thoughts – and you know that I love you, my eternal Father.   AMEN

Daily Reading

O Lord, our Lord,
  how majestic is thy name in all the earth!
Thou whose glory above the heavens is chanted
  by the mouth of babes and infants,
thou hast founded a bulwark because of thy foes,
  to still the enemy and the avenger.
When I look at thy heavens, the work of thy fingers,
  the moon and the stars which thou hast established;
what is man that thou art mindful of him,
  and the son of man that thou dost care for him?

                                        Psalm 8 : 1-4

In the Morning

O God, I don't want to be lazy, and stay in this comfortable situation. Stir me to the delights this opening day offers — to its freshness, its cleanness, its challenges.

Hold this day all loving home-makers —— and ——
all true friends —— and —— and ——
all young lovers —— and —— and ——
all grown grey in the service of others —— and ——

Deliver us from anxiety about what today holds — since all is known to you, and you hold us in your keeping. Where evil is attractive to us, make the good and true even more winsome, I pray. I would spoil none of this day's opportunities, this day's human relationships, but bring them whole and good to you at nightfall.

I bless you for the fulness of life here in time; and for the assurance of a yet richer life beyond the experience of death — by reason of the resurrection power of Jesus my Lord. I give you thanks for the strong certainties of the Christian faith, brought down to me by good men and women.

Bless your Church in all the world, speaking in many tongues, ministering in many ways. Keep her members faithful to you, through Jesus Christ — faithful to each other in their undertakings. We do not all think alike, we do not all worship alike — but we all love you, and we all serve you. Give us to know the wonder of co-operative loyalty, sweet tolerance and eagerness. So beckon us on — yet keep company with us as we move forward. AMEN

In the Evening

O God, if I have been led on by faulty impulses today, forgive
me now.

If I have failed any whose trust I held, forgive me now.

If any looked to me for help, and found it not, forgive me
now.

If I have carried around a dour expression, forgive me now.

If I have been in any degree full of self-pity, forgive me
now.

And with your forgiveness, I can seek my rest — and on the
morrow begin again.

I can learn from my mistakes, and not be utterly cast-down.
Keep me, I pray.

And when the new day comes, O Lord, keep me mindful
of the promises I have made;

when success blesses my honest efforts, let me not be puffed-
up with pride;

keep me, O Lord, from my worst enemy, which is most often
myself. For Christ's sake.   AMEN

Daily Reading

Paul writes of God : 'He has delivered us from the dominion
of darkness and transferred us to the kingdom of his beloved
Son, in whom we have redemption, the forgiveness of sins. He
is the image of the invisible God, the first-born of all creation;
for in him all things were created, in heaven and on earth,
visible and invisible, whether thrones or dominions or principalities or authorities — all things were created through him
and for him. He is before all things, and in him all things
hold together.'   Colossians 1:13-17

TWENTY-NINTH DAY

In the Morning

O God, creator of all, who first brought this world into being with the words 'Let there be light!', you are still giving that command with each new day. I rejoice in your power to command both light and darkness. Hold me equally at your gracious command this day, though you have given to me as a person the power to refuse to co-operate.

Bless all those who go out into this new day, desiring to do your will in the world – all who rise, as I do, renewed by sleep, strong in the sense of your nearness, and your gracious power.

As the night sounds of nature give way to sounds man-made, let me not be so caught up in rush and tear, that I make no room for your voice. And when I sense what is your will for me, let me not try to excuse myself from action.

Let me use my body well today – my mind, my possessions – as one belonging to your world family. Let me handle my money – the earning and the spending of it – to your glory, mindful of the needs of many others in this world. Bless all the new tasks I undertake today; the new people with whom I have dealings. Let all I do and say witness to you in every-day affairs. For Christ's sake.   AMEN

In the Evening

O God, I praise you for your creative power in this day now drawing to a close – in the lives and the affairs of men and women here and everywhere.

    I find strength in the fact that you are never off-duty, since
        you are moved by eternal on-going love;
    I find strength in the fact that I am not the first to know
        that love in action, in my life;

I find joy in remembering the relationship of Jesus to you,
    as he lived this human life here.
Father, take what has been good in my talk with others
today, and let it live in their memories;
    what has been good in my serving today, and let the world
        I inherit be a better place;
    what has been good in my secret thoughts, and help me
        express it in true and happy living.
Now the darkness shuts out the great world about me, and
this room seems a little world of its own; but nothing can
shut me from your care, as I relax into sleep. Keep all dear
to me, here and afar, and bring us again to the new day,
eager and assured. In Christ's name, I dare to offer this
prayer.   AMEN

Daily Reading

The wilderness and the dry land shall be glad,
    the desert shall rejoice and blossom;
like the crocus it shall blossom abundantly,
    and rejoice with joy and singing.
The glory of Lebanon shall be given to it,
    the majesty of Carmel and Sharon.
They shall see the glory of the Lord,
    the majesty of our God.
Strengthen the weak hands,
    and make firm the feeble knees.
Say to those who are of a fearful heart,
    'Be strong, fear not!
Behold your God!'   Isaiah 35: 1-4

THIRTIETH DAY

In the Morning

O God, give strength to my will, and joy to my senses this day, that my witness to you may be strong and winsome.

Let pride be done away, as I remember whose I am, and whom I serve;

let imagination stir itself to reach out beyond the limits of my setting;

bless your great Church in all the world, and all who give themselves to her ministry.

Grant to all who nurse the sick of body, and the mentally disturbed this day, your wisdom and courtesy and patience, I pray;

Grant to all who teach little children, especially the handicapped and dispossessed, the human qualities they need, I pray;

Grant to those who live in lands overrun by war and famine and hate, the special courage they need and the wisdom to find a new way of life.

We are all your children; we are all dependent on you;

we are a mingling of ignorance and knowledge;

we are all uneven in our allegiance, full of feelings that at times betray us.

Bless those in authority over us in the country, and the community, in our places of work and service. Let good relationships prevail; guide into better ways those who use the tools of protest, revolt, and strike. Guide all whose purposes are set on building up the good, rather than in the often more dramatic act of pulling down that which others have built.

Bless all who are low with discouragement;

bless all beginning new tasks today, with some trepidation;

bless all coming towards retirement, reward them with the knowledge that they have served well.

And keep me this day, in my own tasks, though few will know what they are, and how well I do them. Show me how

to do things today, in your good spirit, and not in my own.
For Christ's sake.   AMEN

In the Evening

If anything I have done this day has hurt another, forgive me,
O God – and let me take good care that it never happens
again.

If anything I have passed on to another in conversation this
day has been unfair, untrue, forgive me, O God – and let me
take care it is not repeated.

If any long-past resentment has been allowed to come to
the forefront of my mind, and engage my conscious thought,
forgive me, O God, for Christ's sake.

So may I come to my sleep, unashamed, forgiven and trustful.   AMEN

Daily Reading

If I speak in the tongues of men and of angels, but have not
love, I am a noisy gong or a clanging cymbal. And if I have
prophetic powers, and understand all mysteries and all knowledge, and if I have all faith, so as to remove mountains, but
have not love, I am nothing. If I give away all I have, and if
I deliver my body to be burned, but have not love, I gain
nothing.

Love is patient and kind; love is not jealous or boastful; it
is not arrogant or rude. Love does not insist on its own way;
it is not irritable or resentful; it does not rejoice at wrong;
but rejoices in the right. Love bears all things, believes all
things, hopes all things, endures all things. Love never ends.

                                            1 Corinthians 13: 1-8

In the Morning

O God, I have come to know you, and to trust you, through the words of good men and women of earlier times –
    in the scriptures of the Old and New Testaments;
    in the witness of the Church the world over;
    in daily contact with some whom I respect;
    in daily worship and instruction in the congregation;
    in the reading of books that have come into my hands.
I marvel that you have so many ways of making your love known to me; that your eternal purpose is always one of love and truth.
    Forgive me, if I have harboured a grievance against any;
    forgive me, if I have shown intolerance to any;
    forgive me, if my unhelpful moods have spoiled any relationships.
And let me move amongst people, as a person whose whole life belongs to an extra dimension, vital faith – under divine direction daily;
    so may my home be a happy place, where you are honoured;
    so may my work be faithfully done, as though you see all;
    so may my hope in the worthwhileness of things good and true live on.
In Christ's name, I find courage to ask these blessings.

AMEN

In the Evening

Never morning wears to evening, but some hearts do break, O God – bless now all for whom this has been a taxing day, a dark day:

all involved in accidents of any kind;
all made aware of some family shame;
all faced with involved medical reports;
all whose dear one faces death and the new life.

Remember this day those for whom I feel I can do little myself — let me do the best I can, with the understanding I have for —— and —— and —— and ——

Hold them each in the hollow of your hand;
and give to those who tend them clear vision, steady skill;
keep them today, body, mind and spirit.

In this world there is a great deal that I find confusing — but nothing too hard for you to unravel and control. I depend on your love and wisdom.

Now that this month is at an end, I think back over the way it has led me, and I give thanks for your wondrous keeping, your sustaining joy and purpose. Let me carry over into the new month none of the faults I have faced in myself, none of the prejudices, none of the foolishnesses. So may I live anew, and to your glory. AMEN

Daily Reading

Praise the Lord!
Praise the Lord, O my soul!
   I will praise the Lord as long as I live;
   I will sing praises to my God while I have being.
Put not your trust in princes,
   in a son of man, in whom there is no help.
When his breath departs he returns to his earth;
   on that very day his plans perish.
Happy is he whose help is the God of Jacob,
   whose hope is in the Lord his God,
who made heaven and earth, the sea, and all that is in them;
who keeps faith for ever. Psalm 146: 1-6

PRAYERS WITH
BIBLE READINGS
FOR FIVE SUNDAYS

Reading

The people who walked in darkness
  have seen a great light;
those who dwelt in a land of deep darkness,
  on them has light shined.
Thou hast multiplied the nation,
  thou hast increased its joy;
they rejoice before thee
  as with joy at the harvest,
  as men rejoice when they divide the spoil.

Isaiah 9:2-3

In the Morning

In every generation, O Lord, people have loved you and found joy in your service. Let us do that in an even greater sense today, because we have been led out of the semi-darkness of the Old Testament, into the light of the New. Christ has promised joy to those who are his disciples – a joy that no man can take from us. Let me know that joy today as I go to worship – a joy that no one can give me, and no one take away. This is something deeper than mere jollity – it is established as a gift in the whole of my personality.

So I would sing the hymns of joy this day, in the congregation, and in my own secret heart – and give thanks to Christ who overcame the hold of death and darkness, and established his Church on the reality of the world's first Easter morning.

Let this shining wonder spread far and wide today; bless all ministers who raise their voices to proclaim it. For Christ's own sake.   AMEN

FIRST SUNDAY

In the Evening

Draw near in a most real sense, O Lord, to all who assemble for worship this night – some are perplexed, some full of thanksgiving;
  some are deeply aware of sinfulness;
  some lack the assurance of approach that Jesus gives.
Grant your guiding hand to all who prepare the order of service –
  all who choose hymns and anthems;
  all who sing in the choir;
  all who receive the offering of the people.   AMEN

SECOND SUNDAY

Reading

Jesus said : 'The Spirit of the Lord is upon me,
because he has anointed me to preach good news to the poor.
He has sent me to proclaim release to the captives
and recovering of sight to the blind,
to set at liberty those who are oppressed,
to proclaim the acceptable year of the Lord.'   Luke 4 :18-19

In the Morning

I rejoice that Jesus made his way to worship in the village
where he grew up; and wherever he happened to be, in manhood. He has set us all an example in this — let me follow his
example today.

I would not surrender to the temptation of bodily tiredness;
I would not let my attendance be subject to my moods;
I would count it a privilege to worship, as Christ did.
Bless especially all with responsibility for worship today :
let the hymns be well led and meaningfully sung;
let the prayers said together be sincere and real;
let the Scriptures speak with your own authority.
So may we all return home forgiven, renewed and blessed.

AMEN

SECOND SUNDAY

In the Evening

The day ends, O God, and the darkness closes us in. Be with us, as we assemble for thanksgiving and praise. Let the actions of our lives match the words of our lips – it is so much easier to speak than to live. But you have power to enable us to do this well and gladly.

Bless especially all for whom this has been a day of sorrow, a day of pain, a day of strain and unhappiness. Bless all who have had to report for work today, in order that others might be free to rest and worship.

I rejoice that as the earth turns others who love you in other lands will join in your praise. This strengthens my own faith now. AMEN

Reading

One Sabbath he was going through the grainfields; and as they made their way his disciples began to pluck heads of grain. And the Pharisees said to him, 'Look, why are they doing what is not lawful on the sabbath?' And he said to them, 'Have you never heard what David did, when he was in need and was hungry, he and those who were with him: how he entered the house of God, when Abiathar was high priest, and ate the bread of the Presence, which it is not lawful for any but the priests to eat, and also gave it to those who were with him?' And he said to them, 'The sabbath was made for man, not man for the sabbath; so the Son of man is lord even of the Sabbath.'   Mark 2:23-28

In the Morning

You have led me to exchange the holiness of the Jewish sabbath for the holiness of the Christian Sunday, O Lord, and I rejoice. This day reminds me of Christ my Lord risen triumphant from the dead, and I rejoice.

Let his spirit guide me into its proper use, that I may bring honour to your holy name, and knowledge and refreshment of spirit to my week's work ahead. Whatever my task, enable me, O Lord, to do it well.

Let the words of the prophets and psalmists, the apostles and letter-writers come with fresh loveliness to me today. Let the fellowship of worship in the congregation be real and strengthening, the preaching of the word be stimulating.

AMEN

THIRD SUNDAY

In the Evening

The noise of the busy world outside sings as I assemble with others to worship, O God. You know what this day has held for me – you know my motive for coming to worship this night, and all my secret needs.

Forgive me for my sins of the week past – if ever I have acted or spoken a lie; if I have been more concerned with my own selfish needs than with the needs of others; my own plans than the plans of others.

And abide with me this night, O Lord, as really as Jesus went in company with those who walked to Emmaus at nightfall. For his name's sake.   AMEN

FOURTH SUNDAY

Reading

Again Jesus entered the synagogue, and a man was there who had a withered hand. And they watched him, to see whether he would heal him on the sabbath, so that they might accuse him. And he said to the man who had the withered hand, 'Come here.' And he said to them, 'Is it lawful on the sabbath to do good or to do harm, to save life or to kill?' But they were silent. And he looked around at them with anger, grieved at their hardness of heart, and said to the man, 'Stretch out your hand.' He stretched it out, and his hand was restored.

Mark 3 : 1-5

In the Morning

O God of men and women in health and sickness, I rejoice that Jesus came demonstrating your compassionate heart. I rejoice that he understood how things looked to a man in trouble, cut off from his power to work and earn his livelihood. I rejoice that Jesus always put things in their proper perspective – that the keeping of a rule never took first place with him before a sufferer's need. I rejoice that he had the courage to do the things that seemed right to him, without concern for his own popularity with the crowds.

Bless all who gather for worship in our Church today. For Christ's sake. AMEN

FOURTH SUNDAY

In the Evening

O God, there are many things in this life that are frustrating
and beyond my power to explain; there are many things that
are painful and hard to care for in medical terms as we know
them; there are many people handicapped in body and mind.
Bless all who set their skills to compassionate service in
Christ's name.

   Let us worship this night in sincerity and truth;

   let us link ourselves with those who suffer;

   let us remember always the leadership of Christ.

Let the words of Scripture, interpreted by the preacher, come
clearly to our hearts and minds, that practical effort may result.
Here and now.   AMEN

FIFTH SUNDAY

Reading

The women who had come with him from Galilee followed, and saw the tomb, and how his body was laid; then they returned, and prepared spices and ointments.

On the sabbath they rested according to the commandment.

But on the first day of the week, at early dawn, they went to the tomb, taking the spices which they had prepared. And they found the stone rolled away from the tomb, but when they went in they did not find the body. While they were perplexed about this, behold, two men stood by them in dazzling apparel; and as they were frightened and bowed their faces to the ground, the men said to them, 'Why do you seek the living among the dead? Remember how he told you, while he was still in Galilee.' Luke 23 : 55-56; 24 : 1-6

In the Morning

I bless you, O God, that Sunday by Sunday I am reminded of the first glad Easter Day — the first day of the week, by the Jewish reckoning — when Jesus burst the bonds of death and rose triumphant. I remember the faithful women to whom this glad news was first revealed; who first ran eagerly to share it with others. Let my experience of the risen Christ today be as real and let me share the wonder of it as eagerly.

Forgive me that ever I have grown casual and lost the wonder of my faith. AMEN

In the Evening

O God, let your light fall on earth's dark places, I pray; let your joy of the risen Christ fall on despair and fear; banishing both, in his power. Let the issues of injustice and war be done away; let men learn how to live in the power of the resurrection. Where hopelessness dwells withering the bright future, let your new life come.

We know that you are more ready for these good changes than we to ask. Give us the earnest desire to have your Kingdom come, your will done.   AMEN

SIX GRACES FOR USE
AT TABLE

Grace at table is one of the oldest acknowledgements of our human dependence on God, and interdependence with our fellow-men and women.

My friend Frances Russell offers more than a whimsical note in her 'Grace for the Comfortably Off' :

'God bless this food
Superfluous,
And may it put
No weight on us. Amen.'

In this hungry world, we truly pray –
O God, we bow before this meal, mindful of the needs of others, thankful you meet our own.   AMEN

God, receive our thanks for the gifts of many seasons, and the service of many hands.   AMEN

For good food and good fellowship, we give you thanks, O Lord.   AMEN

O God, ever generous in the nourishment of our bodies, nourish our spirits too, we pray.   AMEN

O God, we bring you our thanks for food, fun and fellowship here together.   AMEN

As once Christ blessed the loaves and fishes, bless now our use of all these dishes.   AMEN

PRAYERS WITH BIBLE READINGS
FOR FESTIVAL DAYS

CHRISTMAS DAY

In the Morning

O Father, it is hard to realize that this wonderful morning is with us again!

The children have looked forward to it for long enough, and we adults have made preparations!

But Christmas is more than any of us can do –
it is your miracle gift of incarnation;
it is the means by which you tie heaven and earth;
it is the widening of love, for Christ's sake.

Let none within the bounds of your world Church this day fail in joyous realization of what this morning means – and come to worship;

Let none within the bounds of your world Church this day
let our carols and our hymns ascend sincerely;
let the New Testament story reach us with freshness;
let the peace you offer come to this sad world, because first we glorify you.

Save us from excess this day, in giving and receiving, in providing and eating – because for so many of your children it is a time of need –
bless all who organize and disperse what gifts we give;
bless those who gather little children to hear the story;
bless those who ponder the deep, adult meaning of this season – no mere child's story.

Let orphans and refugees, the bereft and lonely, the poor and dispossessed, glimpse something of your exceeding love and joy today – through the hospitality of our hearts and homes.   AMEN

CHRISTMAS DAY

In the Evening

I praise you, O God, for all the joyous meaning of this day — a Saviour born, a Son given, a Redeemer come amongst us.

I bless you for the ministry of a stable bed in a small town on the fringe of big affairs — Bethlehem.

I bless you for the safe-keeping of your Son as he was carried into Egypt, a refugee.

I bless you for the simple setting of his youth, and young manhood, the home in Nazareth.

I bless you for the hallowing of all family relationships — which Christmas is; for all who have gathered round me to make this a happy day of fellowship, good memories, gifts given and received. Let me carry over its spirit into the other days of the year. To the honour of the young king born.

AMEN

Daily Reading

In those days a decree went out from Caesar Augustus that all the world should be enrolled. This was the first enrolment, when Quirinius was governor of Syria. And all went to be enrolled, each to his own city. And Joseph also went up from Galilee, from the city of Nazareth, to Judea, to the city of David, which is called Bethlehem, because he was of the house and lineage of David, to be enrolled with Mary, his betrothed, who was with child. And while they were there, the time came for her to be delivered. And she gave birth to her first-born son and wrapped him in swaddling cloths, and laid him in a manger, because there was no place for them in the inn.

Luke 2 :1-7

NEW YEAR'S DAY

In the Morning

O God of new beginnings, you have brought me to this day
— with thanksgiving, and renewed love and trust.

I look back over the old year gone — its many surprises, its
many good experiences;

I remember with sorrow some of the stupid things that I
allowed to creep into its days;

I rejoice that your forgiveness has matched my sinfulness
and ongoing need.

Let me step into the New Year unhindered by the past, eager
to live to your glory, in your world, in all sincerity:

take the strength of my body, and the thoughts of my mind,
and the aspirations of my spirit;

take the accumulated experiences that the years gone have
given me, and use them to new purpose;

take the friendships of the days, and beautify my conversation and routine tasks as I start again today.

Let the everlasting values of the Kingdom of Christ be
mine of choice, and the loving obedience of my heart be
unquestioned, my Father, this day.   AMEN

In the Evening

Already the wonder of a new beginning is upon me – without your forgiving love, O Lord, I would sink in despair. So often my actions fall below my beliefs, so often I am guilty of good deeds undone, good opportunities unrecognized; good resolves unrealized. Forgive me, O God – and let me stir myself to see that this casualness does not persist in my daily life. You are always ready to forgive – and to grant a new beginning to the truly penitent – but let me not take this for granted, as an easy thing. Bless at this time of renewal all known to me and loved by me —— and —— and —— and —— and —— Those I am in close touch with; those I am out of touch with. All are known to you; all are within range of your caring. Let the life of Jesus challenge us all to better living through the days of this New Year.

As we start out, let us be more honest in our prayers than in the past, more trustworthy with our possessions, more generous with our money and our energies and skills. For Christ's sake, who lived always so well.   AMEN

Daily Reading

Paul writes: 'Examine yourselves, to see whether you are holding to your faith. Test yourselves. Do you not realize that Jesus Christ is in you? – unless indeed you fail to meet the test! I hope you will find out that we have not failed. But we pray God that you may not do wrong – not that we may appear to have met the test, but that you may do what is right, though we may seem to have failed. For we cannot do anything against the truth, but only for the truth . . .

The grace of the Lord Jesus Christ and the love of God and the fellowship of the Holy Spirit be with you all.'

2 Corinthians 13:5-8, 14

FIRST DAY IN LENT

In the Morning

O Lord, I do not come to this new day, as to a lash for my
spiritual laziness — I come with wonder in my heart for all that
it truly means:
   guide me through its days to a new and deeper spirit;
   guide me to a new sense of responsibility in all I have;
   save me from slack indulgence and selfish planning;
   deliver me from grudges and resentments;
   grant me courage and perseverance as I go through these
      days.
O Lord, you have set me to live in this place and time; you
have enriched me by the Christian experiences of many men
and women before me:
   let me profit by their discoveries, by their mistakes, their
      love;
   let me take time to consider what values are my choice;
   let me develop in these days a new responsiveness to you.
So may this time be no casual keeping of a festival set in the
Church's calendar, but a real experience of renewal and loving
purpose.   AMEN

In the Evening

O God, my Father, I need constantly a true sense of propor-
tion — so many things become part of my life without due
thought. You have given me this time of Lent, for recollection in truthfulness and reality. I can so easily bluff those
about me with words that come easily to my lips — but all my
inmost motivations are known to you. And because you are
my eternal Father whose desire for me is only the best and
finest, I put away all pretence, and speak my heart truly in
this prayer.

And what I pray for myself, I pray for those tied to my life and sympathies — members of my family —— and —— and —— and —— friends and acquaintances —— and —— and —— and —— neighbours —— and —— those to whom I owe a debt of gratitude —— Bless all ministers and priests and nuns and deaconesses and teachers of religion, at this season — let it be a rich time for them, and shared unhurriedly. Enable them each truly to renew vows taken in days gone; and to understand new depths of their allegiance, not only with their minds, but in their hearts.

If life's claims press heavily, enable us to lean upon you, O God, with more lively dependence. So let us triumph, in Christ. AMEN

Daily Reading

He was despised and rejected by men;
    a man of sorrows, and acquainted with grief;
and as one from whom men hide their faces
    he was despised, and we esteemed him not.
Surely he has borne our griefs and carried our sorrows;
    yet we esteemed him stricken, smitten by God, and afflicted.
But he was wounded for our transgressions,
    he was bruised for our iniquities;
upon him was the chastisement that made us whole,
and with his stripes we are healed.

Isaiah 53 :3-5

GOOD FRIDAY

In the Morning

From the beginning, O God, this has been a day that weighed
heavily on human hearts – a day of cruelty, of suffering, of
bewilderment.

Bless with vision all for whom it is no special day.
I rejoice that I can look beyond the bounds of these few
hours;
that I can welcome light shining in utter darkness.

I try to link myself with those disciples who stood faithfully beneath the cross on Golgotha – the women there, most
faithful of all;

but I cannot think of that happening as they thought of it;
so much has been written of it, since – so much spoken;
I cannot see that sad day in isolation.

To me, it is all part of the long pattern of redemption, the
triumph of Easter Day, with men and women of faith, re-
made, re-energized in spirit.

I marvel at the spirit of Christ shown on Good Friday;
I marvel at his attitude to those who crucified him;
I marvel at his care for those two alongside him, and those
beneath – his mother Mary, and John his friend.

I bless you for the courage and generosity of Joseph of
Arimathea, who lent his new tomb – that Christ might know
dignity in death;

give faith to all who must themselves face death, this day;
give faith to all who face death alongside those they love;
give faith to all who fear death, and what it can mean –
and let them see Christ triumphant, in your good time.

Let the words that we speak, the prayers we offer, and the
hymns we sing be real, despite our limited understanding of
what this day involves.

GOOD FRIDAY

In the Evening

O God, my Father, I can hardly wait to have this sad day pass into another, on the way to resurrection and triumph; yet I cannot spare this day from the calendar of the Church. Help me to use it well and meaningfully.

I confess that my loyalty does not always stand up to tests;
I confess myself as impulsive often as Peter;
I confess that I too have betrayed my Lord, like Judas;
I too have been frightened by public opinion, many a time;
I too have shut myself away like the disciples, and bolted
    my heart's door to save an awkward meeting.
Help me in my turn to rejoice as they rejoiced;
And as eagerly to share my deepest convictions abroad.

So may this day of remembrance issue in finer discipleship — to the glory of Christ, whom I dare to call 'My Lord and my God!'   AMEN

Daily Reading

All we like sheep have gone astray;
    we have turned every one to his own way;
and the Lord has laid on him the iniquity of us all.
He was oppressed, and he was afflicted,
    yet he opened not his mouth;
like a lamb that is led to the slaughter,
    and like a sheep that before its shearers is dumb,
    so he opened not his mouth.
By oppression and judgement he was taken away;
    and as for his generation, who considered
that he was cut off out of the land of the living,
    stricken for the transgression of my people?
And they made his grave with the wicked
    and with a rich man in his death,
although he had done no violence,
    and there was no deceit in his mouth.   Isaiah 53 :6-9

EASTER DAY

In the Morning

O God, my heart joins with countless others to share in the wonder of this day:
  to cry with them, 'Christ the Lord is risen!'
  to carry new hope to the fearful and defeated;
  to renew my own discipleship to Christ.
Let the hymns of praise on my lips today and the words of prayer rise sincerely and gladly to you;
  I remember how Christ said, 'Because I live, you too shall live';
  I remember how graciously he made himself known to Mary;
  I remember the strength of those who knew him for the risen Christ.
Enable me to put away all things tied to death, despair and defeat; and to live in the triumphant power of Jesus Christ, Lord of all:
  when I come to difficulties too great to face alone,
  let me realize that since the first Easter Day, all is changed;
  when my courage flags, may I remember all who have been renewed by faith in the risen Lord.
O Lord, enable me to practise the things I most deeply believe – not to speak of service and live selfishly; not to speak of love and fail in it; let me not bring discredit to the faith I profess.   AMEN

EASTER DAY

In the Evening

O Lord of life, let me remember your infinite greatness, your mercy greater than your power; so let me trust you utterly, in life and in death. Let discouragement never merge into defeat – let me have life, as Christ intended, and life abundant. So let me face each day – whatever it brings – and come to the day's end calm and more than conqueror over circumstances.

I ask for your keeping of all dear to me —— and —— and —— Bless their goings out, and at this time, their comings in. In mercy look upon them, forgive their sins, and renew their allegiance to you. Surround their lives with firm, good friends and neighbours, strengthen their standards of behaviour, that they too may bring glory to your name. Speak to them in the quietness of their churches, their homes, this night. This, I ask humbly, for your love's sake.   AMEN

Daily Reading

But Mary stood weeping outside the tomb, and as she wept she stooped to look into the tomb; and she saw two angels in white, sitting where the body of Jesus had lain, one at the head and one at the feet. They said to her, 'Woman, why are you weeping?' She said to them, 'Because they have taken away my Lord, and I do not know where they have laid him.' Saying this, she turned round and saw Jesus standing, but she did not know that it was Jesus. Jesus said to her, 'Woman, why are you weeping? Whom do you seek?' Supposing him to be the gardener, she said to him, 'Sir, if you have carried him away, tell me where you have laid him, and I will take him away.' Jesus said to her, 'Mary.' She turned and said to him in Hebrew, 'Rabboni!' (which means Teacher).

John 20:11-16

WHITSUNDAY

In the Morning

O God, I give thanks for the powerful meaning of this day —
  linked with the experience of those first at Pentecost;
  linked with the promise of Christ himself, whilst here;
  linked with the experience of countless Christians now.
Banish from my life all dullness, all dreariness, all lack of
power to live :
  whatever my tongue, let it witness to your power;
  whatever my skin colour, reassure me of your leadership;
  whatever my failures in the past, renew my faith today.
You have made of one blood all men and women of this
earth :
  help us to reach out and support each other;
  help us to show pleasure in each others' skills;
  help us to witness to your Fatherhood, as we can.
Spirit of Christ, coming as the wind, where it listeth, mighty
as flame,
  purify my every motive, move me gladly into service;
  take charge of my mind, as well as my feelings;
  let me love and praise you as a whole person.   AMEN

In the Evening

O God, I bring my praise for your keeping this day, as I lie
down to sleep :
  I do not deserve all your mercies;
  I cannot fully realize your providence;
  I fail to fathom your gifts of peace and joy.

Speak to me afresh this night, through the Scripture records
of long ago, when your Spirit was first abroad in the world:
    in the early days of creation, when darkness was overcome;
    in the days of the prophets, when people had much to
        learn;
    and when people were gathered, of one mind in one place,
        at Pentecost.
Speak to me through the experience of men and women in
my own day, and through good books and papers available:
    let their witness cause me to renew my own discipleship;
    let their eagerness not leave my own behind;
    let the joy that comes to them be my own discovery.

                                        AMEN

Daily Reading

Luke wrote: 'I have dealt with all that Jesus began to do and
teach, until the day when he was taken up, after he had given
commandment through the Holy Spirit to the apostles whom
he had chosen. To them he presented himself alive after his
passion by many proofs, appearing to them during forty days,
and speaking of the kingdom of God. And while staying with
them he charged them not to depart from Jerusalem, but to
wait for the promise of the Father, which, he said, "you heard
from me, for John baptized with water, but before many days
you shall be baptized with the Holy Spirit."

So when they had come together, they asked him, "Lord,
will you at this time restore the kingdom to Israel?" He said
to them, "It is not for you to know times or seasons which the
Father has fixed by his own authority. But you shall receive
power when the Holy Spirit has come upon you." '

                                      Acts 1:1-8

ALL SAINTS DAY

In the Morning

O God, I waken to this day that reminds me that all ages and
types of people have a place in your Kingdom:
   people without haloes as they live on this earth;
   people whose days are full of secular things;
   people belonging to many different denominations.
I rejoice that the saints of your Kingdom are being fashioned,
not just in faraway times, and in faraway places:
   it is their utter self-giving to you which marks them off;
   it is their love of truth and service of others;
   it is their translation of the gospel into living terms.
I am glad to have known a good number of saints myself,
men and women both, praising you above all else in life,
showing love to you above all else:
   they have shown me the meaning of simplicity;
   they have shown me the beauty of humility;
   they have shown me the enduring nature of love.
Let me add my contribution of devotion to those from whom
I have received so much, so often in this life—through books,
words and actions:
   help me not only to serve you in safe, comfortable tasks;
   let me rise to tasks needed, that involve some hazard;
   lead me in the way of gentleness and reconciliation.
So let me tread in the footsteps of your saints. In the same
Spirit.　　　　　　　　　　　　　　　　　　　　　　　AMEN

In the Evening

As this full day closes, I bring you my praise, O God, for all the good things it has held – for new experiences, for additional service, deepening truth;

I rejoice that Jesus came into our earth-life, to show us its beauty and wonder, its love, and everlasting worth; to lift us out of the commonplace into the sublime;

Hold in your keeping this night those who are in my thoughts just now – they would scarcely call themselves saints, though they serve you, and love you here and now;

Forgive us for anything that has marred our discipleship this day – and send us to sleep assured that in your power it need not happen again.

Gather us all in now, as night covers our side of the earth.

Grant us your peace that passeth all understanding. In the name of Christ. AMEN

Daily Reading

Paul, a servant of Jesus Christ, called to be an apostle, set apart for the gospel of God which he promised beforehand through his prophets in the holy scriptures, the gospel concerning his Son, who was descended from David according to the flesh and designated Son of God in power according to the Spirit of holiness by his resurrection from the dead, Jesus Christ our Lord, through whom we have received grace and apostleship to bring about obedience of faith for the sake of his name among all the nations . . . To all God's beloved . . . who are called to be saints.

Romans 1 :1-7

PRAYERS
FOR SPECIAL OCCASIONS AND
PARTICULAR OCCUPATIONS

O God, I praise you for what I know of this great world — for the darkness that gives way to light at your word; for the men and women who share it with me joyously; for wild creatures, their habits and colours and songs and calls.

I bless you for my small share in making things beautiful;
  for new life that rises from my planting;
  for flowers that add colour and fragrance;
  for patterns and shapes, an added boon of variety.
I bless you for those who long ago planted trees —
  for fine twigs filigreed against the sky;
  for leaves of many shapes and colours;
  for streams and rivers and ponds and sea coasts.
I bless you for mountains and hills, for plains and valleys —
  so great is the diversity of your creation;
  so full of purposes joined in life;
  so rich in opportunities for work and rest.
O God, let me be a faithful steward of these things entrusted to my care; let me share my delight in them, with others, in the name of Jesus who loved all nature about him.   AMEN

A Prayer before Shopping

Gracious Father, give me good judgement as I go out into the shops today — save me from extravagance and from coveting what I cannot rightly afford:
  all nature is beautifully clothed — the hills, the beasts, the fish, the birds;
  let me be as suitably clothed, in my work-time and play-time;
  let me not fall to flattery, or to behaviour unsuitable to my age group.
Today, O God, give me patience when shop-tired, to keep on searching —
  even if it means another day, in another place;

and above the clothing of my body, let me concern myself
    with the clothing of my mind and spirit;
let me make room for meditation and count it no waste to
    expend time and money in bookshops and libraries.

AMEN

A Prayer of a Young Mother

I marvel, O God, that you have given into the keeping of two
inexperienced people, this lovely little child —
    that you have blessed it with a soft, pliable body;
    that you have set within a waking mind;
    that you have lighted within an eternal spirit.
Let me never forget to nourish all three — that a whole person
may love you, and serve you in the home, and later in the
wide world.
    Bless the meals we share, the air we breathe;
    bless the fun of bath-time, and story-time, and prayer-
        time;
    bless the walks and rides and swings that spell joy.
Strengthen our interdependence as a family — showing love
and consideration for each in turn, caring for the personal
gifts of each.
    In sickness and health, bind us close together;
    in school and home, at work and play, bless us together;
    in our worship at Church, and Sunday school, enrich us.
And so let us keep learning as long as life lasts, and keep
serving as long as we keep learning — praising you to the last
day on earth.

AMEN

A Nurse's Prayer

I thank you, O God, for my vocation — following in the tracks
of the great healer. I bless you for what I know of his healing
ministry in the towns and villages about Palestine:

he is the inspiration of countless numbers of us who tend
the sick;

we have been trained for this ministry – help us to keep up-
to-date in our techniques;

give us the tender touch, endless patience, and sense of
lightsome fun we need;

enable us to deal with patients as individuals, one by one,
each with a special background.

Where there is anxiety, let us bring a compassionate understanding, where there is pain, the gentle touch, where the task
is long drawn-out, a goodly courage;

so let us minister wholeness to the broken;

so let us offer comfort to the frightened;

so let us bring peace to the mentally distraught.

All these things I ask in the name of Christ my Lord.   AMEN

Setting about Spring Cleaning

O God, I am surprised to find how dusty things can become
just by being left alone; forgive me if I have been inclined to
put off this task;

now that I have done with excuses, let me set about it
gladly;

now that this fine day has come, let me do the job tho-
roughly;

let my duster and mop reveal hidden beauties gradually
forgotten.

Keep me safe as I clamber into high places – let me make
sure that my steps are set securely on the floor, before I mount
to fix curtains and drapes:

if new furnishings are due, let me match and replace with
skill;

let me not be tempted to expense above what is called for;

let me keep my house-pride within proper Christian
bounds.

I love my home; I love my family to enjoy it, and say so;

I like to be able to offer hospitality to others as the days come and go:

 let the spirit of Christ dwell here – as in the home of Mary and Martha;

 let me not be so concerned for things that I embarrass people;

 let my home-keeping praise him who had no home after Nazareth;

Let him find a welcome across my threshold; now and for ever. AMEN

Going Out to an Entertainment

O God, who took rest at the end of the world's creation – I rejoice in this time of leisure. Bless me as I make preparations to go – attending to garments and transport, checking time, and arranging for company. Let it be good, refreshing fun. Bless us as we travel to and fro – as we share the experience, and together learn some new thing, respond to some unknown beauty.

Bless all who contribute to the entertainment – the result of years of tuition, and discipline and self-giving. Reward them with our sincere response; and where there is occasion, with our applause. Keep their standards high; continue to extend their gifts and graces; and send us all home thankful for this time of sights and sounds shared. AMEN

Prayer of a Woman Living Alone

O Lord, I am but one of many, who for one reason or another, live alone. This way of life has some advantages, you know, some disadvantages. Keep me constant in cooking myself real meals and in setting them out temptingly, though I am all alone.

I have friends in and out, as often as I can manage – but with only one pair of hands, it can't be very often.

Some of us, you know, live alone, of choice;
some of us because of family estrangement;
some of us because we have inherited property.

Grant your special support to all who are nervous alone; to all isolated from other homes about; all who are embarrassed by the cost of keeping things going; all who, in frailty, cannot manage a garden any more. Give good judgement and courage to those of us who suspect that the time has come for a change in living arrangements. Bless our thoughtful neighbours – and help us to be neighbourly in turn. For Christ's sake.   AMEN

A Typist's Prayer

O Lord of life, let me live well and eagerly this day – faithful in the discharge of my duties, particular about my moods and my appearance, as I work alone or with others :

I have confidences to keep – let me be dependable;

I have neatness of work to consider – let me take pleasure in it;

I have time to spend on each – keep me prompt with promises.

Bless this day my relationships within the office; keep my conversation above gossip; let me be punctual in my comings and goings; respectful of my seniors, proud of the good name of my firm.

You know how I live and where; you know how much I earn;

help me to handle this secular matter, as a sacred charge,

let me be a good steward of all that passes through my hands.   AMEN

A Prayer for Creatures

Gracious, ever-active Creator, it is wonderful that you have given us the companionship of creatures.

Their colours and habits are full of interest; their trust wins our desire to feed and play with them.

Bless all friendly cats and dogs and creatures about our home – let us take good care of them – especially during holiday-times.

Bless this day all working animals – horses on roads where so much wheeled traffic is; ponies that bear children to school or to play.

Bless all who ride spirited mounts, let them consider their animals, feed, water and groom them well.

Bless all captive animals, in zoos and circuses – and let those who show them be merciful and patient.

These things I ask in the name of him who rode an ass into the crowded city of Jerusalem, amidst shouting and excitement.

AMEN

A Motorist's Prayer

O Lord of all who travel at speed in this day of motors, let me join them with care:

    thoughtfully taking my place at the wheel;

    starting up my engine once more;

    gathering speed to set out on my chosen direction.

Men and women have always travelled, but these days our roads are full of dangers, full of careless people, some scarcely sober;

    let me take good care to be responsible;

    let me do what I can to keep my vehicle roadworthy;

    let me refuse the temptation to drive boastfully.

And give me patience with the slow to cross; the deaf, and blind, the absent-minded; and keep my eyes alert for animals and birds;

    let me look out for children running after balls, or riding;

    let me think imaginatively as I approach others, at speed;

    let me use my car for others' pleasure, as well as my own.

So let me go out without anxiety, and return with satisfaction, and thankfulness.

AMEN

A Teacher's Prayer

O Lord of all true learning, bring me to my task today, eager and well-prepared.

I have my training and my past experience,
but I need your gift of perception and patience;
I need your loving concern for young growing minds;
there are so many new needs in maintaining discipline;
I must know hourly what things matter, and what do not matter.

Deliver me, O Lord, from mental laziness – keep me up-to-date;

enrich my fellowship with other teachers;
strengthen my co-operation with parents and guardians;
sustain my cheerfulness as term wears on, and I tire;
refresh my body, mind and spirit, in holiday-times.

And when success crowns my efforts, let me not forget to thank you.   AMEN

A Prayer for One Newly in Hospital

The sun rises, O God, and life in this busy place begins – bless all who bear responsibility here – and all new at the work;

I pray especially for doctors and nurses, for ward-maids,
I pray for all who work behind the scene – X-ray technicians,
I pray for those who serve in the laboratory and office,
I pray for ambulance-drivers and administrators of this hospital year in, year out.

I haven't thought much about many of them until now – forgive me;

help me to co-operate with those concerned for my welfare;
help me to keep cheerful, and save me from self-pity;
bless my people at home, and all concerned for my health;
bless those who remember me, in prayer, with letters and cards.

So may the day soon come, if it is your will, when I return home better for this experience, and more compassionate in my regard for others.

In the name of Christ the healer of bodies, minds and spirits.   AMEN

A Prayer on Going to Church

As I come to your house of worship today, O God, grant me reverence;
    I love to know myself part of an immense company on
       earth;
    I love to be aware of your presence, as I hush my heart;
    I would not love orders of service, more than I love you;
    I would not cherish doctrines that damn true worshippers;
    I would not serve creeds more than my care for your
       Kingdom.
Let me hold to the faith handed me by saints and apostles, martyrs, good men and women, ever open for new revelation from you;
    I cannot forget the world beyond my pew, because I live in
       it;
    I cannot forget the human frailties that beset us all;
    I cannot be the kind of person I would be, without your help.
    I humbly seek that help;
    Open the Scriptures to me freshly today;
    Let me grasp the fact that your will is everlastingly good,
       and that your promises are promises.
So mould me as part of my congregation, my community, my country, O Lord.   AMEN

In a Time of Sadness

O God of infinite love and compassion, you know how things are with me just now — you know the ties that link my life with others:

and when times like this come, I find support in my friends;
I am not the first to walk this way of confusion and concern;
I am not alone in this experience, here and now.
Save me from looking at once on the dark side; keep up my
hope;
let me think clearly, and know what it is best to do;
save me from any hasty word, that can only spell hurt.
And when I have done all, let me accept the fact that here
there are problems which know no solution, pains for which
there is no cure.
I remember that Christ shed tears at the grave of Lazarus;
let me not be ashamed of any I might be moved to shed.
Keep fresh my memories of blessings received;
and let my hands be ready with what practical service I
can render just now, just here.   AMEN

Prayer on Holiday

O God, it is lovely to lay down my work for a brief time of
relaxation and renewal —
to see fresh sights and to meet new people;
to keep different hours and rise later each morning;
to plan each day and take unusual meals.
I do not forget that whilst I relax, some must still work;
enable me to show courtesy to those who serve me;
enable me to pass nothing of beauty and interest unnoticed;
enable me to refresh my mind and spirit as well as my body.
Let me find my way to Church on Sunday, to worship as my
custom is;
keep safely, I pray, all those I love at home;
save me from reckless expenditure on my own pleasures;
and bring me home again, the better for the 'break' in my
daily routine.
In the name of Christ who bade his own close friends 'Come
apart!'   AMEN

A Speaker's Prayer

O God, you know how I must soon honour my promise to speak to these people. Clear my mind, and guide my preparation in this brief time that remains, that I may stand before the company serene, natural and glad;

keep my memory clear, my choice of words fitting;

save me from any conscious display of superiority;

give me good voice control, that the deaf and old may hear well.

Let me keep to the point throughout, that it will be a pleasure to listen, and grant to me some sparkle of fun. I would not take myself too seriously. And let me be fittingly clad, that what I say may linger longest in the minds of those listening – without distraction. So may something of truth, beauty and refreshment be added to life today.   AMEN

A Student's Prayer

It seems, O God, a wonderful thing that for this definite length of time in my life, I am able to study, and to associate with others who do the same. I give thanks for this opportunity denied to some.

Keep me diligent in my private preparation, attentive to lectures;

keep me honest in my purposes, retentive in memory, clear in reasoning, natural in bearing.

Whilst I live in this world of students, keep me aware of the outside world;

in the hours I am away from home, keep me faithful to those who care;

when tasks are difficult, give me courage, and humility in the hour of success and acclaim.

I dedicate to you all my faculties, that your Kingdom may be served – it is your gift, though you use human co-operation.

Help me to go on learning, as long as life lasts – and to go

on day by day living the truths I learn. For the sake of Christ
who is all truth.   AMEN

A Counter Prayer for Those Who Serve

O God, the world seems different from this side of the counter.
Make me ready to do well today the thing I have to do —
    let me fully know my stock;
    let me be pleasant and approachable;
    let me show patience when matters become involved;
    let me speak courteously, however provoked.
People can still at times show themselves unreasonable —
    Jesus knew that — he sold goods to customers;
    he made things to match needs;
    he knew the satisfaction of a satisfied customer.
Let me likewise take a pride in good wares and in good ser-
vice. For his sake.   AMEN

Confession after a Quarrel

Eternal Father, I'm ashamed to have behaved like this. Forgive me. It was a good deal my fault — and I know better. I
shouldn't have reacted as I did.

    Let me now lay aside my pride, and be the first to mend the
breach. And let me do it right away — not wait to excuse
myself out of it. For Christ's sake, restore our relationship,
who taught us to forgive, even as we are ourselves forgiven.

                                                                       AMEN

Prayer of One Caring for Little Children

Gracious God, I rejoice that I have been entrusted with young
lives —
    each is so different, each so charming;
    but, at times, each can be sorely exacting;

I need more than a fondness for them – I need love.
Give me patience too, with the endless questions asked –
   especially those difficult to answer;
   let me be as honest and as simple as possible;
   let our relationship of trust be firmly based.
I give thanks for picture-books, paints and brushes, and all
creative fun –
   for plants and trees and pet animals;
   I give thanks for imagination exercised at play;
   for seaside sands for ball games and building.
Over the years, let me handle well my share in character-
building. In the name of Christ who gathered little children
about him.   AMEN

A Prayer of One Bedridden

O God, my Father, day follows day without much change – my
body holds me here, but I have things for which to give
thanks –
   my bed, with its clean linen and blankets;
   my pillows, with their supporting ease;
   the familiar pictures on my walls;
   the window bringing me light and view;
   my books on the bedside table;
   my vase of flowers;
   the benison of hot water,
   and the blessing of clean garments.
Accept my thanks for the miracle of medical science;
   for the tenderness of those near me;
   keep me unruffled when the unexpected occurs;
   strengthen me in my solitary times;
   deliver me from down-heartedness;
   let those who visit me find reward;
   bless all whose state is worse than mine;
   support me in the dark, wakeful hours;
   give me a continual sense of your presence.

So let my hours of day and night know praise and gratitude.

AMEN

A Prayer of a Missionary

In this land are many things, O God, that I have had to get
used to – but many people whom I already love.

Life here begins early. Let my first thoughts on waking be
turned towards you, before the many claims of the day lay
hold on me.

I rejoice that you have called me to this work;
I give thanks for all who have helped me answer my calls;
I give thanks for those who have laid foundations here.
Bless my colleagues this day, I pray. You have made us such
different personalities – but with a common allegiance to you.
Strengthen our respect.

When the climate is trying, keep us patient;
when bodies weary, keep us faithful to our charge;
when problems loom, let us not take ourselves too seriously.
Bless all at home, who continue to support our mission; all
who pray and give; all who write and remember to send us
equipment.

And when furlough at last comes, hold us in the hollow of
your hand, that we may contribute something of lively worth
to others. For Christ's sake.

AMEN

A Book-Lover's Prayer

O God, whose truth comes in so many ways – I rejoice in
books and magazines :
among the many available, let me choose well;
I am indebted to authors, illustrators, publishers, book-
sellers;
I am indebted to reviewers and especially to my reading
friends.
Help me to a developing understanding of life, a delight

in things good and true. Guide all librarians and deliver them from ruts of routine:

bless those who give their lives to writing; quicken their minds;

keep their standards of undertaking high;

bless their own reading and use of imagination.

And when manuscripts are returned unwanted, keep their courage high; and keep them modest when success blossoms for them. So may hours of interest and enjoyment be shared, and truth and goodness and beauty be spread abroad.   AMEN

A Birthday Prayer

Lord of life, I cannot believe that this day has really come. It seems so short a time since I last celebrated. Bless all my friends who remember me this day – all who call to greet me, all who phone, all who send me cards.

This year has held some specially good things – I recall them now with gratitude;

this year has held some surprises – I go back over them to marvel or to chuckle;

this year has seen a development in some of my interests – I want to go on trying;

this year has also brought me some difficult hours – I thank you that I have not been wholly alone.

And as this new year opens out, let my faith grow stronger and more natural, day by day; let my usefulness as a person mingling with others be more real. Forgive me for the foolish things I allowed into the year past; give me better sense in the year ahead – and strength to 'live more nearly as I pray' – for Christ's sake.   AMEN

A Social-Worker's Prayer

O God, you know that a lot of my time is spent in dismal settings; a lot of my thought is given to problems, and dealing

with puzzled people. Show me how to live well and joyously,
that I may have experience to share.

Give me patience with the self-willed and foolish;

give me tenderness with the deceived, the hurt;

give me a helping hand for the despairing, the lonely.

Save me, O God, from wholesale condemnation, from intolerance, from powerlessness to establish bridges over chasms
of distrust. Keep me alert to new techniques, new advances in
understanding shared by the experts.

Let me remember always how much people matter in your
sight;

let me devote without selfish thought all that I am and
have;

let those who have begun a better way know your strength
to keep them at it. Now and always.   AMEN

Prayer for a Marriage Morning

O God, I can't believe this happy day – so long desired – has
really come. I bless you for this great and mysterious gift of
human love:

keep us both today, from this earliest moment;

when we are each alone; when at last, we are together;

hallow our service of marriage, shared with dear ones;

let our feasting and fun be wholesome and good;

bless our leave-taking – and our honeymoon travel.

O God, bless all our home-making plans, as we build up a
new relationship. And in dark times and bright, let us be
aware of the presence of him who blessed with his presence
the wedding-feast in Cana.   AMEN

A Prayer on Retirement

Creator of heaven and earth, looking back on each new thing
to call it 'very good', I have known that same feeling myself,
at times. Through the years, I have had some good days, some

unforgettable experiences. I have worked alongside good colleagues, and have turned out some good work.

Now the time has come to retire —
it has always seemed afar off;
it will call for some adjustment.

Now that I am to have more time to dispose of as I will, bless my home; bless my dear ones there; bless our time spent together — our meals, our outings, our friends who come to enjoy our hospitality. Bless our hobbies; and keep us from turning in upon our own affairs more than is healthy. Let us spend some of our new leisure giving others a helping hand.

Strengthen our relationship with the Church; there are many opportunities for happy service, now that I am for the first time really free. Let me use them well and serve without thought of position or recognition. In the name of Christ my Lord. AMEN

A Gardener's Prayer

O God, it is lovely to realize that your world of work and human life began in a garden — I can understand that being your choice. In every garden up through the long years you have given to men and women their own Eden.

I bring you my thanks for the soil I tend;
for the digging I do, the seeds I sow;
for the trees others have planted,
for the endless joy of colour and fruitage, O Lord.

I bless you for the variety the passing seasons bring; for the numerous forms of garden life, and endless expectation, O Lord. Let me prove a good steward of your soil, of your seasons, of your sustained creation. And make me ready to share flowers and fruits with others who have none. AMEN

Prayer for a Celebration

O God, who has made us for joy and fun, as well as for

serious undertakings, you have given us in our ordinary lives
occasions for festivity.

You know our approach to this day – long expected;
you know our secret plans – made with much thought;
you know who will share the special hours of this day.

I bless you for every such celebration in the past – and my
memories; I bless you for those who have helped to make
each worthwhile.

Hold us all in the hollow of your hand this day;
let our exchange of experiences be interesting;
let our conversation be without malice or injury.

So let the hours pass for us richly, leaving true satisfaction.
Bless any unable to be of our happy company, through age
or untoward circumstance.

And guide us all as we separate once more.   AMEN

A Prayer before Opening My Bible

It is easy to overlook the daily value of this book, O God,
because I have known it so long –

because it can't rightly be read straight through;
because it is a progressive revelation;
because it is not a book of science in a scientific age.

I give thanks for all the types of literature it uses – poetry,
history, story, fable, song, letter, etc.

for its concern with your will, above all;
for its beauty of language, and witness to the good and
    true and enduring.

In the early days of the race, men and women had to find
their way without this wonderful book;

in the first days of Christianity, too;
accept my thanks for scribes, scholars, translators;
for all who have given their lives to bring it to me.

I pray for an alert and reverent mind as I turn its pages –
for a readiness to avail myself of the best reading-aids in my
language today.

Strengthen the world-wide work of the Bible societies;
the interest of those who give to their funds;
the devotion of those who continue with translation till all
   may share this book.   AMEN

A Musician's Prayer

O God of many voices, I bless you for this world in which I
live – for its many sounds. I rejoice in its birds, and streams,
and winds, and mighty seas;
   I give thanks for folk-songs and lullabies saved from the
      childhood of the race;
   I give thanks for psalms and songs fashioned by people
      long before my time;
   I give thanks for the great composers whose genius is still
      available to me;
   I give thanks for the many types of instrument that men's
      skills have evolved.
Countless times music has led me to a sense of your almighty
presence – countless times it has lifted my heart into a new
dimension of truth.
   Let me use well my capacity to present here, for the joy
   and strengthening of others, my share of music;
      mingling the new with the old. To your glory O God!
                                                            AMEN

A Prayer of the Lonely

O God, this great universe seems greater than ever today – my
insignificance at times presses in on me:
   I feel out of touch with things and people;
   I seem unable to bridge over differences;
   I seem to face each day very much alone.
This feeling I have has more to do with my moods than
with my geographical setting – I sometimes feel loneliest
when I am in the crowd;

forgive me for feelings of self-pity;
forgive me for thinking I am unique;
enable me to reach out to others, especially those who seem
lonely too.

And let the words of Christ lay hold of me with a glorious
reality : 'Lo, I am with you, even unto the end of the world.'

AMEN

A Traveller's Prayer

O God, this is a wonderful world that you have made – and
I am thrilled to be setting out to see something more of it :
bless my preparations – my passport, my visas, the injec-
tions, when the travel is into strange lands;
bless me in my choice of itinerary, my choice of company,
my choice of season;
bless my selection of shoes, clothes, bags – all so important,
if I am to travel without cares;
bless my days of reading and note-making in preparation
– but most of all the spirit in which I set off;
help me to accept people as I find them, to show respect,
and have no superiority about skin colour or language.

And when I have gathered much of loveliness and interest,
enable me to share my finds freely with those at home lacking
this experience. And let me live with greater usefulness, tolerance and love, because of my travels, for your sake, Lord
of all life on this great earth, and of all people.   AMEN

A Prayer of a Housekeeper

O God of order and seemliness, each day brings me many
routine tasks; each day brings me the need for bedmaking and
cleaning and meal-making.
Let me do these things with a lively imagination;
let me derive satisfaction from doing these things well;

let those within my family know more of the dignity and joy of living because of me;

make me a good steward of my housekeeping purse;
save me from thinking I need everything advertised;
save me from wastefulness, or forgetting the needs of any.

I love my open windows, my open doors; the precious little things I have gathered with the years; the pictures and furnishings given me by family —

let me tend well my garden and my pot-plants and vases;
let me take pleasure in providing music, books and talk;
let my home minister to others good hospitality and fellowship, now and always.   AMEN

A Prayer of One Handicapped

O God of movement, you have made this great earth to turn on its axis; the sun and moon and stars to fulfil your purpose unhindered — I love these great things of nature. You have set your streams to find their natural way down slopes to rivers and the sea; you have set the tides to their constant ebb and flow; you have given birds flight, and made animals fleet of foot. Men and women have not lacked the joy of movement — but some of us are handicapped.

Let me not despair because I do not know why;
let me not surrender to self-pity;
let me know courage to match my undertakings.

Bless this day all in my home and in hospitals and clinics and laboratories who give patient hours to research — show them the new ways, if it is your will.

Keep me conscious of your nearness when I am alone;
bless all who try to understand my needs;
and keep some laughter on my lips. For Christ's sake.

AMEN

O God, I'm getting older — the year has come to an end. As I look back for a moment, accept my thanks for all the good it has held. No two years are ever alike; no two sets of friends. Where I have been foolish, forgive me; where I have forgotten whose I am and whom I serve. Accept my thanks for your ministry to me —

through the Church;

through community life;

through government provisions.

And keep me ever mindful of the needs of others, near at hand, and far away. Bring me safely to the end of the way, when all questions at last will be answered, all tears wiped away, and your will joyously done.   AMEN

Also available in Fount Paperbacks

A Gift for God
MOTHER TERESA OF CALCUTTA

'The force of her words is very great . . . the message is always the same, yet always fresh and striking.'

Malcolm Muggeridge

Strength to Love
MARTIN LUTHER KING

'The sermons . . . read easily and reveal a man of great purpose, humility and wisdom . . . in the turbulent context of the American race conflict, Dr King's statements have the ring of social as well as spiritual truth . . .'

Steven Kroll
The Listener

A Book of Comfort
ELIZABETH GOUDGE

'The contents are worth ten of the title: this is a careful, sensitive anthology of the illuminations in prose and verse that have prevented the world from going wholly dark over the centuries.'

Sunday Times

The Desert in the City
CARLO CARRETTO

'. . . we have been in the hands of one of the finest of modern spiritual writers, who helps us on the road of love in Christ.'

Philip Cauvin, the Universe

Also available in Fount Paperbacks

BOOKS BY C. S. LEWIS

Reflections on the Psalms

'Absolutely packed with wisdom. It is clearly the fruit of very much reflection . . . upon one's own darkness of spirit, one's own fumbling and grasping in the shadows of prayer or of penitence.'

Trevor Huddleston

Miracles

'This is a brilliant book, abounding in lucid exposition and illuminating metaphor.'

Charles Davey, The Observer

The Problem of Pain

'Written with clarity and force, and out of much knowledge and experience.'

Times Literary Supplement

Surprised by Joy

'His outstanding gift is clarity. You can take it at two levels, as straight autobiography, or as a kind of spiritual thriller, a detective's probing of clue and motive . . .'

Isabel Quigley, Sunday Times

Fount Paperbacks

Fount is one of the leading paperback publishers of religious books and below are some of its recent titles.

☐ GETHSEMANE Martin Israel £2.50
☐ HIS HEALING TOUCH Michael Buckley £2.50
☐ YES TO LIFE David Clarke £2.95
☐ THE DIVORCED CATHOLIC Edmund Flood £1.95
☐ THE WORLD WALKS BY Sue Masham £2.95
☐ C. S. LEWIS: THE MAN AND HIS GOD
   Richard Harries £1.75
☐ BEING FRIENDS Peter Levin £2.95
☐ DON'T BE AFRAID TO SAY YOU'RE LONELY
   Christopher Martin £2.50
☐ BASIL HUME: A PORTRAIT Tony Castle (ed.) £3.50
☐ TERRY WAITE: MAN WITH A MISSION
   Trevor Barnes £2.95
☐ PRAYING THROUGH PARADOX Charles Elliott £2.50
☐ TIMELESS AT HEART C. S. Lewis £2.50
☐ THE POLITICS OF PARADISE Frank Field £3.50
☐ THE WOUNDED CITY Trevor Barnes £2.50
☐ THE SACRAMENT OF THE WORD Donald Coggan £2.95
☐ IS THERE ANYONE THERE? Richard MacKenna £1.95

All Fount paperbacks are available through your bookshop or newsagent, or they can be ordered by post from Fount Paperbacks, Cash Sales Department, G.P.O. Box 29, Douglas, Isle of Man. Please send purchase price plus 22p per book, maximum postage £3. Customers outside the UK send purchase price, plus 22p per book. Cheque, postal order or money order. No currency.

NAME (Block letters)_____

ADDRESS _____

_____

_____